Beginning your Marriage

STANDARD EDITION

John L. Thomas, S.J.

Published by:
Buckley Publications

Excerpts (pgs. 119-127) from the English translation of the *Rite of Marriage* © 1970, International Committee on English in the Liturgy, Inc. All rights reserved.

Excerpt (pg. 63) from *The Velveteen Rabbit*, by Margery Williams reprinted with the permission of Doubleday & Co., Inc.

Beginning Your Marriage - Standard Edition
Copyright © 1980 Buckley Publications, Inc.

SIXTH REVISION

Library of Congress Catalogue No. 80-65486
ISBN No. 0-915388-06-5

Printed in the United States

Buckley Publications, Inc. • 233 E. Erie St. • Chicago, IL 60611

First printing April 1980 — 50,000
Second printing Sept. 1980 — 50,000
Third printing Sept. 1981 — 50,000

Edited by: *The Beacon Group*
Art: *Charles and Margaret Maier*
Layout and Design: *Marylou Draper*

We wish to express our gratitude to the priests and couples of the Cana Conference of Chicago, with special thanks to *Rev. Thomas Hickey, Elizabeth Bannon,* and *Joseph Dunne* for their help with this revision.

*"The well-being of the individual
person and of human and Christian
society is intimately linked with
the healthy condition of that
community produced by marriage
and family..."[1]*

*In the history of the Christian Church,
the need to prepare for marriage
carefully and intelligently
has never been so urgent as it is
today. We are challenged constantly
by the joys and sorrows of the modern
world, and it is no small feat for
marriage and the community to survive
these challenges. Marriage is the
intimate and ultimate responsibility
of the two people who choose to embark
upon this wonderful, yet solemn
adventure together.*

*It is to this responsibility and to
those who willingly assume it and share
in fostering the nobility of marriage
and the family that BEGINNING YOUR
MARRIAGE is dedicated.*

[1]From the opening statement of "Fostering the Nobility of Marriage and
the Family." Vatican II, *The Church in the Modern World* (*Guadium et
Spes*) 1965. Part II, Chapter I, No. 47

TO WALTER

Contents

"I have come that you might have life more richly and abundantly."

SACRAMENTAL COUPLE

Although you cannot pick them out because they have no distinguishing marks, many couples whom you meet have sacramental marriages. Because you are about to become such a couple, it is important to consider what makes a sacramental couple different and special. It is also important to consider the roots and foundation of the sacrament of marriage in Christ's message to love one another.

THE VISION OF LOVE

Christ became Man so that you and I might live a richer, more abundant life. With purpose, He walked the earth talking to His people—answering their questions, healing their wounds, consoling their sorrows, and rejoicing in their happiness. His purpose? To envelop the world in His love and to teach the people about love, freedom, and responsibility. His message? "Love one another. Love one another as you love yourself." His method? To deliver His message of love, reveal the resurrection, and show us how love can bring forth new life. The Holy Spirit, the Spirit of Love, appeared to a small band of men and women and made them the carriers of the love story of Christ. These special people believed in the power and freedom of that love story and became a community ("Church") of love in God. God *is* love: God is a community of love, and the very essence of God is love in relationship. If holy means to be like God, it means to be able to love. It means being like God, a tremendous, passionate lover, committed to the problems of real people in the real world. We are called to spread Christ's message —love one another.

Christ had a vision that made the earliest Christians into a Church and a people and gave them and us a spirit to unite and inspire us. In Himself, He revealed the ultimate meaning of life. He was the Man-for-Others who said startling things—if someone strikes you, turn the other cheek; if a thief takes your coat, give him your raincoat, too. He said that the Christian challenge is to initiate love —to love the unlovable, your enemies, and one another. He revealed the Resurrection and showed us that all growth, all life, comes through dying to self. If we are to live richly and abundantly, we must risk ourselves in loving others, as He did.

The key to life is the leap of faith that leads us to trust and to love. Once we take that leap of faith to trust and to love, we share in Christ's vision of a world without fear, self-interest, or cruelty. He tells us that all people are the children of God and, therefore, brothers and sisters. He challenges us to dream of the world as it could be—a world of peace, justice, mutual concern, and love. He commands us to go forth and share His vision, to do the work of love and transform the earth.

Having accepted the challenge and the command, we must accept the responsibility of the freedom that love inspires. Freedom to love opens avenues of expression and discovery, but that freedom implies responsibility—if we are free to love ourselves and others in the eyes of God, then we must treat that love and that freedom responsibly. We step out of ourselves to make Christ's vision of the world a reality. We become members of the Church (community), a visible group of people who carry this vision. And we are better able to love ourselves responsibly and without self-interest.

The church, therefore, is the formal group of people blessed, challenged, and stuck with the task of exploring the vision of total love—of living it, bearing witness to it, attracting others to it, and bringing it to bear on the needs of every age and culture.

LITURGY AND THE EXPERIENCE OF LOVE

Only those who experience the power of love believe in it and are impelled to do something about it. The role of the liturgy is to continually form the love community by steeping us in the vision of love, by presenting the Gospel story again, and by helping people experience love. The Christian liturgy is based on the reality of God's grace and each person's need to become a lover. It tells us who we are, dramatizes the important events of our salvation, and nourishes us with the word of God.

Liturgy tries to make us understand and experience the fact that we are all brothers and sisters in Christ. Scripture tells us of one who looks in the mirror but, turning away, soon "forgets what manner of man he is." With today's frantic pace of living, it is so easy to forget love, slip into self-centeredness, and become totally absorbed in our own worlds. In the liturgy, as we listen, pray, speak, sing, and eat together, we find our true identities. We acknowledge that we must return to God through our fellow man.

Christ and His church and people are the great Sacrament, that is, the great symbol and cause of redemptive, altruistic love in the world. Seven related signs put us in touch with God's love and also are called sacraments. "A sacrament is an outward sign instituted by Christ to give grace." Sacraments are special, ritual moments wherein we can open ourselves to God's love.

We need to stop thinking of sacraments in a mechanistic manner. Some people still think that when we go to confession, God, nudged by St. Peter, looks down, points His finger, and zaps grace into us at the moment of absolution. That is not the way it is. Theology tells us God is changeless, always loving, always present. Change takes place in us through the sacraments. It is a qualitative change; it is an intensification of love, a quickening of faith, and a stirring of emotions toward a firmer dedication to God and our fellow men. Sacraments are meeting points, encounters in which we are nourished and challenged by a deeper realization of God's presence and grace.

We receive all our knowledge and all the information that stirs our emotions through signs and symbols—words, pictures, touch, sound. We can only communicate with one another through signs and symbols, and God can only communicate with mankind through symbols and signs.

Sacraments are symbols or signs; they work with the power of signs and symbols, and this power is real and deeply human. Signs and symbols carry power even over time and space. Christ existed; the events of Christ took place. When we are put in touch with them symbolically in sacramental moments, they carry the power to transform us, if we open our minds and hearts to this encounter with His love story.

MARRIAGE AS A SACRAMENT AND SYMBOL

If there were no such nation as the United States, the American flag would still be a beautifully designed piece of cloth, but it would not be a symbol that carried meaning and power. To be a symbol, a flag must stand for a country, its people, and its heritage.

If there were no Gospel and no Christian people, marriage would still exist (as it did for centuries before Christ), but it would not be a sacrament—a symbol that carried special meaning and power. Sacraments have meaning only in context. In a sacramental marriage, Christ and His church are that necessary context.

A fully sacramental marriage is one in which the partners believe in Christ and His Gospel so deeply that faith shapes their values, influences their attitudes, and motivates their behavior as they risk and commit themselves to begin (and constantly work at) the ongoing process of a unique, permanent, and exclusive love relationship. A fully sacramental marriage is one in which each strives to be present to the other with an unselfish growth-producing love that might even be sacrificial and heroic in character at times. A fully sacramental marriage helps you fill each other's needs and call forth the best in each other.

Secure in and sustained and nourished by their relationship, the partners seek to direct this high order of "creative" love toward their children and all those around them. They dedicate themselves to and proclaim the kind of faith-rooted marriage they have entered (and are striving to perfect) in a public, religious ceremony that identifies and announces their marriage as a special, conscious attempt to relive the story of Christ's love in their own lives. Because of Christ's love and grace and because of their faith, the couple's marriage is not only a good human relationship but is also a symbol, cause, example, and further instrument of Christ's creative, growth-producing, redemptive love. Such a marriage becomes a sacrament.

CEREMONY IS NOT SACRAMENT

The religious marriage ceremony itself does not magically produce a sacramental couple. If they do not build on a faith commitment in their lives, if they never explore what their marriage means and how it challenges them, two people are in a sacramental marriage only technically. The process is meaningless because the sacrament and ceremony of marriage is a special dimension of the marriage relationship only when born of a couple's convictions and of their openness and commitment to Christ's challenge to love.

•*What do you mean, born of their convictions?*

What each individual person believes shapes the quality of his life, and a couple's beliefs strongly shape the character of their marriage. Two committed Christians share beliefs that give a special dimension to their marriage.

•*What do you mean by special dimension?*

Let's be clear: The point is not that all sacramental couples are better. If by heritage, training, or life experience, a Buddhist, humanist, or Hottentot couple reaches a significant level of generosity and a spirit of service, they might easily be "better" than a name-only sacramental couple. The point is not that sacramental couples always act with great nobility. They may flounder and fail and have a long way to go just to act decently. The point is that sacramental couples should act on a different set of values and motivations: They seek to live in the context of the Gospel. They are called to a vision and moved by a spirit that can make them more fully human.

For example, John and Alice have been married for nine years. Her father has just died, and they are confronted with the question of whether her mother should come to live with them.

JOHN: "It's not what we planned, but we'll make it work."

ALICE: "We'll have less privacy, but she'll help. She's always been very active."

JOHN: "I'll help her move some furniture; she'll be more comfortable with her own things."

ALICE: "We'll let the kids know and make sure they have a positive attitude."

Now, let's listen to Peter and Susan, our Christian, sacramental couple.

PETER: "It's not what we planned, but we'll make it work."

SUSAN: "We'll have less privacy, but she'll help. She's always been very active."

PETER: "I'll help her move some furniture; she'll be more comfortable with her own things."

SUSAN: "We'll let the kids know and make sure they have a positive attitude."

"Hold it," you object. "The second couple is saying exactly the same things as the first couple." You're right! And that's the whole point.

Sometimes the "sacramental" couple acts exactly like any mature, generous, and loving couple. Being good, intensely loving, and fully human is the point of sacrament and the whole purpose of Christianity. That good and loving couple, John and Alice, might be Buddhists, Hindus, or humanists. They might be living the Gospel without ever having heard of it.

Well, if that's the case, some might object, why bother with faith and sacrament? Simply because all of us need all of the help we can get. Some people, some couples, never grow into intense lovers, attain greatness of spirit, or become fully human. For most of us in our culture, Christianity frees us to be fully human. Christ makes it possible; faith in His vision of life gives us the security to risk loving unselfishly.

Why do you keep emphasizing "becoming fully human?" What does that mean? Humans, who are free to shape their futures, have the potential to be more wise, more just, more patient, more caring, more fully human. This is the goal of Christianity.

St. Irenaeus said, "Man fully human is God's greatest glory." St. Paul meant it when he said, "Put on the Lord, Jesus Christ." To be like Christ is to do what He did— become human. For believers, Christ is the ideal, the model, the paradigm. To the extent that we become more wise, more generous, and more loving, we become more Christ-like, more holy, and more like the "Man-for-Others" in whom divinity and humanity were united.

Have you ever read an essay or a chapter in a textbook, found it difficult or confusing, and suddenly come upon a crucial sentence or definition that clarified the whole thing and made the pieces fall into place? For the sacramental couple, *Christ is the key,* the answer to the mystery of existence, the light that gives meaning to life, the key that unlocks their personalities and sends them through the zone of fear and pride and selfishness and frees them to be fully human.

The sacrament of matrimony begins when a couple stands "In the sight of God and before the face of this company" and declares, "We take each other...'til death do us part." Their love relationship does not begin at that moment. They have been in love for many months. What, then, does the ceremony do?

It proclaims, describes, and dedicates their relationship. Through it, the couple makes their love a public symbol rooted in Christ. They become a sacrament. If one could hear all the levels of meaning contained in the vows they speak, it would sound awesome and glorious.

"All that I am, whoever I am to become, I give to you. I want to discover myself with you and through you. I will always strive to summon forth the best that is in you. I will minister God's grace to you through my love presence.

Whatever befalls us, I pledge to mingle my life intimately with yours, to live, love, and grow...together forever; to form a new love community to serve our children, our neighbors, our fellow men, and our God."

To the congregation, they say:

"We believe with you in the glorious Christian vision...the impossible dream that says if we pour our lives out for each other, we will possess them more richly. We have the courage to try to imitate the Gospel love story in our lives. We want you to look at us, to be inspired, to take heart, for we are willing to hazard ourselves in the deep faith that this vision is true, what life is really about, and the way we will find fulfillment here and hereafter.
We do all this as part of the Christian community and we need your help, support, advice, discipline, encouragement, and prayers to make this dream work. We are sacrament to each other and to all of you."

To the extent that any person can enter into, touch, and shape the life of another, you are invited to do just that in marital love—to assume responsibility for the growth and destiny of your partner, to call forth the best that is in him or her. He is your task; she is your enterprise. In marriage, God's grace and Christ's love are focused and concentrated in you. You are the contact point. You, through your love, bear Christ's love to your partner. You are sacrament to each other.

If the message of Christ's love is to have its full impact, it will come through sacramental people who make it come alive. You become sacrament to each other by surrounding your partner with your committed love—with the care and encouragement he or she needs to grow.

THE SCHOOLS OF LOVE

Becoming a person takes place through a series of environments or schools of love that begin in infancy and end only with full maturity. An infant knows nothing but himself in his early days. It takes him months to figure out who mama and papa are. He is preoccupied with himself. He takes, demands, and cries for the things he needs to survive. Slowly, after several years of love—warmth, safety, nourishment, cuddling, praise—he begins to trust. Subconsciously he concludes, "They take so much time and trouble with me, they must like me. I must be lovable." He begins to realize his self-worth, gain confidence, and open himself to interaction with others. The family loves the infant into the first stages of personhood.

During adolescence, acquaintances, teachers, peer groups, and best friends provide a new environment of love. People who are not family and who owe nothing are attracted and offer friendship. The child learns that he or she is good and appreciated, wanted, and needed and that he won't be rejected even if he fails. He dares to give to others—to be loyal, to share, and to serve. This is the second school of love.

ADVANCED SCHOOLS OF LOVE

Couples move to an advanced school of love during courtship and marriage. They gradually leave "you" and "I" behind to think of themselves as "we." As mutual trust grows, they become more open, revealing themselves more deeply. Vague thoughts, partially formed dreams, and confused insights become more clear as they try to sort them out, put them into words, and share them.

Partners who discover themselves in a Christian marriage can discover much more. Confidence, mutual support, and effort help them grow in selflessness. They call forth the best in each other; they discover Christ's imprint in each other; and they stand astonished that God should have made them so and that He made them for each other.

MOST EFFECTIVE SCHOOL OF LOVE

Marriage is a most effective school of love because it provides special circumstances, motivations, and challenges to make love grow. The excitement of sexual attractiveness, the desire to please, the warmth of psychological intimacy, the security of being fully loved, and the stimulation of the partner's responsiveness all facilitate loving. The partners find the hard lesson of "dying to selfishness" is made much easier in marriage. They are led, enticed, encouraged, and challenged to become more absorbed in each other, until they find that "to love the other as the self" is not only possible, but enriching.

In good marriages, people who have experienced this growth are able to transfer the experience—to risk and give themselves to their children and to others around them. A young man and woman who believe in the "Christ-view" of reality do not, when they marry, simply accept and acknowledge a love relationship that has grown up between them and hope that it will flourish. When they marry, they make a new convenant. They give themselves to each other totally; they commit themselves to care for and cherish each other through all the tomorrows, whatever those tomorrows might hold. They work to create a strong bond, as strong as the love of Christ for His people. They become a sacrament, a living, working representation of Christ's love.

Those in the Christian community who understand look at this couple and see the love of God alive again and revealed in the world—living proof of His love story; living proof of the freedom and responsibility of love.

SACRAMENT TO THE WORLD

Because a sacrament is a symbol, and because a symbol must be visible and public to be effective, a fully sacramental marriage begins with a public ceremony and commitment. A sign must be where people can recognize it and respond to its message.

The couple is sacrament to the world by building the best marriage relationship and family life it can—be it for better—with the wind at their backs and everything breaking for them—or for worse—over a long road dotted with failure and disappointment. But a couple is also sacrament because the strength and insight it draws from the relation-

18

ship should, from time to time, help them carry forth the work of love. Marriage is not an end in itself, but a means, a school wherein the partners deepen the lessons of love and prepare for further involvement in life. Great as marriage is, it must not become an "egoism of two," a selfish refuge from the world—exclusive and unconcerned with people or problems beyond it. Great as the family is, its members can love it too much.

Although some couples may believe that marriage is a final state, it is a process and an invitation. Rich experience awaits you, if you have the courage to become involved. Society—its institutions, its people—has countless needs that require your care. The family is a nuclear community of love that must radiate hospitality, inspiration, and service to all about it. What form this effort takes will depend on you—your interests, temperament, and opportunities. In a fully sacramental marriage some of your love must always spill over to your neighbors.

CONJUGAL SPIRITUALITY

Spirituality requires taking time to pray, to reflect on who you are and what you are for, and to listen for the challenge of God within you. Married spirituality means deep dialogue; it means sharing what you believe. It means occasionally asking yourself, "How are we doing—for each other, our children, our friends, and our families? Should we attempt more? Should we cut down?" Married spirituality means reflecting upon and discussing your Christian commitment.

Married spirituality also means self-discipline. Sometimes self-discipline is chosen, like cutting down on alcohol; dieting to keep your body trim; working on an unruly temper; turning the television set off so you can read and talk; taking time to confront problems and plan. At other times, self-discipline might need only to be accepted, like a limited budget or unpleasant relatives, unusual working hours or a hyperactive child. Self-discipline teaches us to love.

Spirituality means taking the trouble to foster awareness of the Christian dimension in your lives. Perhaps you attend special liturgies that move you and speak to you. Perhaps you take the trouble to find a parish community where you feel part of the Christian people. You might try joining a Christian Family Group or an Encounter group, or taking adult education classes. Pay attention to ritual and decorations in the home, starting with Christmas and Easter and working through the other religious events of the year. You might become involved in church activities— working with young people, the aged, or one of the many communities found in any parish. If the Christian dimension of your life is to be kept alive, you can't get by on what you learned in grammar school. You must work at it and nourish it.

Finally, the sacramental couple is the one that sees the world with a different vision and believes that "those who abide in love abide in God and God in them."

"Love is never boastful, nor conceited, nor rude; never selfish, nor quick to take offense. Love keeps no score of wrongs; does not gloat over other men's sins, but delights in the truth. There is nothing love cannot face; there is no limit to its faith, its hope, and its endurance. Love will never come to an end. In a word, there are three things that last forever: faith, hope and love; but the greatest of them all is love."

I Corinthians 13

Marriage is not commitment to an institution. It is
commitment to a person, a vision and a process.

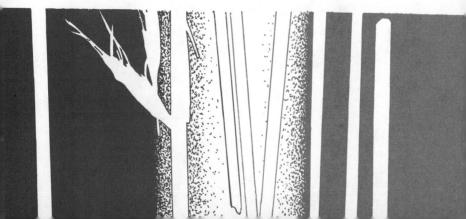

CREATIVE FIDELITY

Whenever Jesus of Nazareth and His followers came to a new town, it was an event. All the people of the countryside gathered to listen, to discuss and dispute, and to find out what He was teaching.

On one occasion, dialogue became quite heated when some Pharisees, learned guardians of Judaic Law, brought up a controversial topic of the day—divorce. One school of thought held that divorce could only be granted for a very serious reason, such as adultery. Another taught that divorce could be granted for almost any reason at all. At the time of Our Lord, Judaism was seriously divided on the question of divorce.

The Pharisees confronted Jesus and asked Him to align Himself with one or the other position. "Where do you stand?" they asked. Jesus replied, "I do not believe in divorce. A man must not leave his wife, nor a woman her husband. Marriage is forever."

"But what about our Law-giver, Moses," they protested. "He allowed a man to divorce his wife." Jesus said, "Moses allowed it *not* because it was a good idea, but because of the hardness of your hearts—your unteachableness at the time."

Often, when Jesus said something strong and potentially inflammatory, the Apostles would panic. They looked at the excited crowd, told them to rest a moment, and pulled Jesus away to talk. "Lord, do You know what You sound like in public? Did You hear what You said about marriage? Who on earth would ever get into that kind of relationship—no loopholes, no escape clauses, no fine print. You mean that's really the way it is between a man and a woman—once you're married, it's forever? If that's so, then it might be better not to marry at all."

Then, one suspects, Jesus smiled and said something like, "At last you understand! My idea of marriage is that it is a glorious, remarkable, extremely difficult, and demanding relationship."

In that very same discussion, a rich young man had asked Jesus, "What must I do to be perfect?" Jesus replied, "Simply give away *all* of your money and follow Me. Come, walk into an indefinite future. Leave behind mother, father, home, family—all the things that mean security. We'll start with nothing but a smile, and we'll prowl the world seeking people who need love."

Of marriage, He implies much the same thing. It is not a matter of entering into an agreement where you know all the terms, demands, and breaking points from the very beginning. Christ says that when you embrace a person, you have no real idea where it might lead. No one can tell you the outer limits of your marital experience. You are walking into the unknown and into the mystery of yourself and your lover.

You simply agree *in advance* to be with a person who moves, grows, wanders, changes, fouls up, and gets into scrapes. If you do this, you can be certain of one thing—it will be an adventure of love and a journey in the direction of the kingdom of God. Total, unconditional acceptance of another person is a dream that God's grace brings to reality.

Permanent, exclusive marriage is a Christian ideal, one of Christ's fundamental teachings about family life. And, discussion of permanence leads us to two questions:

First, why is permanence such an important ideal? Why dedicate yourselves to permanence in an age when so many others are settling for trial marriages, successive marriages, open marriages? Second, how can you build a permanent marriage at a time when divorce has become almost universally acceptable?

Some say marriage should be permanent because church law says it should be, but, that's not a wholly sufficient or satisfying reason. The laws of the church are not arbitrary statements, floating in space: They are anchored in the basic Christian value—to love one another. They have a purpose; they are pointed toward human growth and holiness.

So, the question becomes: Why does the church have such a law? How does a permanent and exclusive marriage serve the cause of love and growth? *A belief in fully committed love and a realistic dedication to a permanent relationship provides a special environment of trust and security that allows people to let go of fears and defenses, to risk and to grow.*

Complete trust and security is not present on the wedding day. The bond of trust grows over time as a couple logs hundreds of experiences in which they count on each other, depend on each other, and are not disappointed or betrayed. But the intentions they have on their wedding day—the convictions deep within them—are important. These chart the course.

25

If the couple really means, "together forever," if they know they are investing part of their freedom, if they are not poised and ready to interpret every problem as disaster (asking, "Is this it? Is this the breaking point? Is this where I'm a fool if I don't bail out?"), then they are truly undertaking the slow process of building a rich and rewarding relationship.

In marriage, "forsaking all others" is a momentous commitment. But the giving up of options is not a negative process; it is simply the natural by-product of freely choosing to invest yourself in your beloved, "Forsaking all others" does not mean that no one else is richer, smarter, sexier, better-looking, or more fun than your fiance. Nor does it mean that you might not meet them on your honeymoon, three weeks later, or three years later. It *does* mean that when others come along, even though you may be attracted momentarily, you will not seriously consider the others as "options," because you have committed yourself to another.

PROMISES AND VOWS

Vows made between two people who truly intend to have a permanent marriage provide certitude and security. Vows tell each partner what they can count on so that they need not negotiate with each other, manipulate one another, or try to attract each other constantly. A couple starts with a firm base of committed love and, from that point, enters their relationship more deeply.

Paradoxically, in a good marriage, *"while never taking each other for granted, the partners take each other for granted."* This simply means that while they must frequently nurture their love with consideration, attention, and imagination, they can also be certain that the love relationship truly exists. They do not have to start from square one every morning. The relationship can stand stress and weather storms. If the partners need to be takers sometimes, they know they have reserves from which they can draw. Above all, each knows that the partner wants the marriage to work and will strive to make it work.

If Ted suddenly remembers at work that he was surly the previous night and wonders if his wife will be home when he gets there, he's not going to get much work done. Or, if George is really late and Mary worries that he might be out with another woman, she will be eaten with anxiety.

If marriage were a continuum of testing, doubting, trying to sell yourself and win the other anew, never trusting promises or the experience of love, a couple would never mature. Children would not be reared; bread would not be baked; bridges would not be built.

There is no such thing as a trial marriage. There can be "trial" relationships, a trial "living together," but never a trial marriage. As soon as you put in the condition, "If it doesn't work out, we'll call it off," you left out an essential element of marriage—commitment.

The basic difference between a typical marriage and a Christian marriage is that people in a typical marriage *accept* the bond of love that has grown between them, formalize it with a ceremony, and hope it will last. Two Christians who "marry in the Lord," commit themselves to create a bond of love, to give themselves totally and without reservation, and to make their relationship work. They have the courage and the audacity to say, "Whatever the unknown, this we will count on. We will adventure together."

ADVENTURE IN PERSONAL GROWTH

"Permanent marriage is an excellent environment for personal growth, for one of the most obvious

ways that people grow is by meeting and over-coming obstacles and challenges, by stretching themselves."

Ellen, a skilled secretary, is 29. At nineteen, she completed two years of college; she has since had eleven different jobs. The longest lasted seventeen months; the shortest, barely nine weeks. Her problem? People—misunderstandings, quarrels, stress. They happen inevitably, and her only solution is to chuck it all and move on. She has yet to understand others' needs and limitations or how to respond to them, and she has not realized her own deep need for constant support and recognition. If she keeps running away, she will never master herself or the situation.

A similar situation can occur in marriage. For example, Jan thinks Paul ought to be less intense, less critical, less worried about money, and less of a workaholic. She invites him, as best she knows how, to explore another dimension of life in which he might be more tolerant, more peaceful, more joyful in the present. But Paul doesn't see it that way; he sees criticism of his values and lifestyle. When things become too uncomfortable, he pulls out and gets a divorce. He looks for someone who will "accept him as he is." By running away, he has spurned an opportunity for growth.

Of course, a permanent relationship alone is not going to solve Paul's problems. No one is defending a merely stable marriage; just staying together wins no prizes. Some couples stay together because they are *conflict-habituated*. That is, they need each other to fight with, hurt, and feed upon. Tension and psychological warfare mark all of their days. Others stay together in *devitalized relationships*. They are just too passive to do anything else. They may share interest in their children and in maintaining their joint property, but the emotionally related dimension of their life together is apathetic and lifeless, a dry wasteland in which nothing grows.

The ideal, permanent, exclusive marriage is a *vital relationship* marked by closeness, sharing, trust, encouragement, support, forgiveness, empathy, and courage —a deep, many-stranded psychological bond that nourishes growth. The most telling argument for permanency is that making such a marriage work fosters the wholeness and maturity of each partner's personality. Sexual expression limited to one person produces a deeper and more concentrated love. Both partners learn and exercise the skills of relating. They must grow in patience, prudence, courage, forgiveness, honesty, self-discipline, compassion —all the strengths of character, or virtues if you will, that make us more human.

Partners in an exclusive relationship share the most intimate and primitive experiences. They share name, privacy, food, bed, nakedness, sickness, hopes and fears, grief and laughter, strengths and weaknesses, secrets, family ties, religious convictions, pregnancy, children, old age, and even death.

EXISTENTIALLY INDISSOLUBLE

The shared experiences of marriage take place gradually over time and within an intimate, secure environment designed to provide a step-by-step, cumulative growth in trust, self-knowledge, and mutual understanding. These experiences foster a deepening sense of "We-ness," the "two-in-oneness" noted in the book of Genesis. In this sense, they are true bonding experiences. By sharing them, the partners develop a level of mutuality and interdependence that no one else can fully fathom. The partners become, as one author puts it, "existentially indissoluble," that is, they have grown to be so much a part of one another that they stay together because they *want* to stay together. Regardless of what others may think, say, or do, they know this is the most satisfying way they can live their lives.

Couples who are successful in developing this binding relationship are not just lucky! Nor are they simpletons with a low threshold of marital expectations. Rather, they are realists. Like most couples, they enter marriage because they feel they love each other so much that they wish to share a life together. But, they also recognize that they enter this partnership as amateurs and that they have much to learn—about themselves, about their partners, and, above all, about the actual, practical demands that their own distinctive partnership may call upon them to fulfill.

Although aware of their own limitations and the unpredictability of future challenges, couples in a successful Christian marriage are absolutely certain about one thing —their loving, unconditional commitment to each other for life. Come what may—disagreements, misunderstandings, poverty, sickness, etc.,—their commitment will never be questioned. Their commitment is the one aspect of their futures they can control—it alone can supply the assured, unchangeable framework within which they can proceed confidently not only to make adjustments and adaptations that frequently are trying, but to safely undertake the tiresome, often threatening task of carrying one another's burdens.

Unfortunately, we, like the startled Apostles, tend to have a negative view of Christ's norm of indissolubility. We see it as an unfair restriction on individual freedom. However, a moment's reflection on human history, both past and present, would quickly reveal the positive, far-reaching individual and social implications of this norm. The great theologian, St. Augustine of Hippo, did not hesitate to identify permanency as one of the major "goods" or "blessings" in marriage. Because it makes clear the inherent sacredness of a partnership that involves the utmost intimacy, delicate self-exposure, and trusting interdependency of two separate but complimentary images of God—each with its own distinctive destiny to fulfill—permanency is "good." Because it assures husbands and wives that their life partnership is grounded upon an irrevocable commitment that is pleasing to God ("What God has joined together, let no man put asunder."), permanency is a "blessing."

American people have always prized marriage very highly. On the average, they are more likely to marry, to marry younger, and to marry more often than people in any other industrialized nation in the Western World. Approximately 96% of the American population tries marriage at least once. Unfortunately, many have not yet learned how to avoid causing each other anguish by taking so many "practice shots." The presumption that a different partner will "make me ectastically happy" may be foolish.

Marriage needs time. Marriage partners need a future dimension so that plans, reveries, and dreams can challenge, entice, and inspire them. They need time to make mistakes and repair them, to fall out of love and back into love more deeply than ever. Can you conceive of a young man saying, "Darling, I need you and want you. The sun rises and sets on you. I cannot live without you. Will you marry me for a year-and-a-half?" The idea is grotesque. The deepest thrust of true love is its permanency.

The final and most important reason for permanency we will mention only briefly here. Marriage, in its fullest sense, is about children. All of our experience and research tell us one thing loudly and clearly: Children grow and develop best in a good, stable, loving family. No other child-rearing system yet devised can truly replace the stable family.

MARRIAGE IS FOREVER, BUT HOW?

At a time when one out of every three marriages ends in divorce, and many of the rest are said to be barely tolerable, how can *you* build a satisfying, permanent relationship? You must realize that you and your partner will change your interests, values, energy levels, looks, etc., in a hundred ways. Your life circumstances will change; society will change. To remain the same—a loving wife or husband—*you* have to change. And, *don't let change in your partner or yourself come as a surprise.* Marriage is a living, dynamic relationship. It must have its roots in friendship and a willingness to change together.

Beware of different growth rates. John has to read and study many things in his job. He meets exciting people, travels a great deal, and goes to high level conferences and seminars. He's growing in status, responsibility, and vision every day. One night he "sees" that Joan is still spelling her way through *True Romances* and thinks daytime TV serials are the height of culture. The thought sneaks into his mind, "Maybe I should have married someone else." *Who's at fault? Both partners.* He for not taking the time and making the effort to "bring her along." She for not being aware of what was happening and making an effort to grow.

Mary loves concerts, lectures, reading. She's involved with the Art Guild, migrant workers, and a theology discussion group. One night she notices Charlie, asleep again, "watching" the same movie for the seventh time. She realizes that he has grown in nothing but paunch since their wedding day. She begins to think, "I could have done better." Same problem. One grows, one doesn't, and both drift apart. "Take me along" is an important watchword in marriage. On the other hand, you also need support systems.

"Isolated couples who have no one but each other to depend on, can come to devour each other like psychic cannibals. They blame the partner for every boredom and frustration and demand that he or she keep them constantly interested, satisfied, and amused. Impossible!

By meeting people, inviting people, caring about people, you work at building a circle of good friends for yourselves as individuals and, more especially, for yourselves as a couple. You need people with whom you can share certain aspects of your life, people who have common interests and values, people you can depend on for help and understanding.

CONNIE'S STORY

"My name is Connie. I'm 55 years old. I've had this face a long time, and I've earned every crease in it. I have a husband, three children, and five grandchildren.

Mac and I have lived a great deal in 30 years. We're together, and we're the best of friends. What about tomorrow? Ask me tomorrow. We've survived lost jobs, World War II, a tour of duty in Korea, a daughter in the front bedroom for two years with rheumatic heart disease, and a teenage son who got into drugs rather heavily. We've prevailed against a sexy widow who had Mac all staked out and against a handsome, lonely neighbor who said he needed me very much.

I'm supposed to tell you about 'creatve fidelity.' Fidelity has been the key to our life together. Being married is never once-and-for-all; it's a challenge every morning, every season.

Most people think infidelity means climbing into bed with somebody. That's the least of it. Sam Green, our neighbor, has been unfaithful to his wife Lucy through ledgers, bank statements, and sales charts. That first concern, that center of attention a wife needs—he gave to his business; Lucy got what was left. Carol Williams, who lives down the street, is what I call a 'married mother.' She's unfaithful to her husband because her children get attention first and constant care. If one of them develops a hangnail, it's a crisis. Bill Williams is just part of the furniture.

I've seen men unfaithful to their wives through their mothers, fishing, and cars, and I've seen women unfaithful to their husbands through their jobs, housekeeping, and even church work. If this 'infidelity' lasts long enough, the neglected partner may well take off as soon as somebody shows some real human interest in him or her, or both may spend dull years just tolerating each other. Creative fidelity, on the other hand, means taking the time to be continually sensitive to the other's needs. It means using imagination to stimulate and interest the partner.

Creative fidelity is really supporting the partner when he or she wants to do something. Like the time Mac wanted to take a couple of courses at the local junior college. Two days later, I was saying, 'Here are some brochures from the college for you. Most of the good things are on Mondays and Thursdays. I'll switch my bowling night to Wednesdays and come over and audit one of those Thursday classes with you.' That's a lot different from saying, 'OK, go if you want to.'

Creative fidelity can also be confronting. Like the time

I got upset at the young couple next door. She had been on the block for only about two months and had already become extremely popular. I began making unkind remarks about her until Mac came in one night and, in his kind and easy way, said, 'Listen, friend, I'm a little troubled about some of the things you've been saying about the Bryans. Maybe we are not being quite fair with them. Let's invite them over a couple of times and get to know them better.'

When Mac wanted to risk our savings to start a new business, I was scared. But I knew he had to give it a try, so I supported him—scared to death inside, but as energetic and enthusiastic as I could be. Between you and me, I think I supplied just the support he needed to make the whole thing work."

"Your slightest look will easily disclose me,
Though I have closed myself as fingers,
You open always petal by petal myself
As Spring opens (touching skillfully,
mysteriously) her first rose."

LOOK OF LOVE

Love is the outreaching of your personality that thrusts you into the heart's concern of another. When you are open, trustful, responsive, caring, and supportive of another person, *Love is you*. Love is the power you have to "reach out and touch somebody." Having done this, you allow that person to trust you, to believe that you will do your best never to be hurtful, and to entrust the building of a relationship to your mutual caring.

Love is giving, sharing, thinking, willing, and doing all those things that allow the recipient of your love to grow and mature as you grow and mature—in a relationship that both of you strive carefully to nurture. In a mature, loving relationship, each partner recognizes and fosters the individuality of the other and the interdependence (not dependence) each has within the relationship. Love is creative and based on the inner strength, love of self, and respect that each person brings to a relationship. To love is to risk disappointment, pain, and loss. Not to love is to risk being alone, isolated, and painfully unfulfilled.

John Dunne's poem "No Man is an Island," poignantly addresses the human need for contact with other people. Alone and isolated on an "island," we become anxious, insecure, frightened, and frustrated. We have no one to reflect our goodness or assure us that we are wanted and appreciated. We are without someone to whom we can give, from whom we can receive, or with whom we can share. We may not even have someone to notice that we are around. We all have the need to love and be loved, to be recognized and accepted.

On the other hand, a certain amount of loneliness is inherent to the human condition. Once we leave childhood and become aware of our ultimate dependence on ourselves and our own resources, and once we become aware of the sobering finality of our existence, even the most unreflective among us is bound to become aware of his or her ultimate aloneness. This basic aloneness, coupled with our equally basic need for others, is an inescapable dilemma of the human condition: Each one of us is autonomous, but none of us is totally self-sufficient.

Some struggle against loneliness by losing themselves in the herd, by conforming to the ways of the masses and becoming carbon copies of everyone else. Others become workaholics, spending all their time in feverish, work-related activity. Still others become wrapped up in the pursuit of transient sexual encounters. All fail in their attempts, because the only cure for loneliness is relatedness and intimacy—love.

To be human is to thirst for meaning, to strive for knowledge—to know and to be totally known. To be human is to move into a hundred relationships in which and through which we are affirmed, valued, and challenged to grow. We must be *for* others, and we must be *with* others. We must be involved in their feeling, caring, sharing, suffering, laughing, growing, and even dying. Our relationships prepare us for the ultimate relationship of which St. Augustine speaks: "Our hearts are hungry, Lord, and they will never be at peace until they rest in Thee."

TO LOVE IS TO RISK

Although love wihin a strong, caring relationship may ease our loneliness, the risk in giving and accepting love is often overwhelming. When we love, we give much of our innermost selves into the keeping of another. We trust that love and that person. And, whenever we trust, we run the risk of being hurt. Those closest and most important to us, those upon whom we are most dependent for support and self esteem, can hurt us deeply. Those closest and most important to you before marriage are mostly parents, family, teachers, and best friends. With marriage, the partner becomes the most significant person in your life. If he or she turns on you, it can be very painful.

Physical nakedness in marriage is more or less taken for granted; the increasing psychological nakedness in marriage is not so obvious or taken for granted. Each partner drops masks and defenses and reveals fears and weaknesses slowly. For example, Tom begins to learn Susan's most vulnerable areas, and Susan soon pinpoints Tom's most tender spots. One day, in argument or anger, he might shout, "You know, I agree with something you once said. You really do have a big nose!" Or she might scream, "Will you ever learn to speak English well enough so I don't have to be ashamed of you?" Both Tom and Susan trusted because they loved, but each fell short of that trust by playing on each other's weaknesses in an angry moment.

On the other hand, although to love is to risk, the pay-off in risking is tremendous. One day Tom, or Susan, or both, can say, "I've exposed the worst in me—sometimes I'm lazy, messy, confused, frightened, overdemanding—yet he (she) desires and prizes me." This deep affirmation of self-worth is heady and liberating, for now Tom and Susan will never need to expend energy playing games.

Whenever your partner reveals weaknesses or fears, mark them "fragile" and deserving of careful handling. No matter how angry or provoked you may be, a cheap shot at these vulnerable areas can be most damaging.

"To love is to be vulnerable. Love anything and your heart may be broken. If you will not risk that, then give your heart to no one.

Wrap it carefully with hobbies, pets, and little luxuries; lock it safe in the coffin of your selfishness. In that coffin—safe, dark, motionless, airless —it will change; it will become unbreakable, impenetrable, irredeemable."

LOVE OF SELF

To be able to love your partner fully, unselfishly, and joyfully, you must love yourself first. Strong, lasting relationships are made between reasonably secure and self-accepting people who like themselves and who know they have gifts to bestow on each other. The best candidates for a fulfilling marital relationship are those who have no absolute need to marry, who are whole and strong enough to go through life alone.

The worst candidate for marriage is the person who says, "I am nothing without you. I can't live without you." If one simply means, "I desire you very much," fine. But if one is saying, "I have no resources without you; you must fill deep personality voids within me; you must make up for all my disappointments; you must make up for all the years my parents didn't love me and in which I was unpopular," then one is bringing little more to marriage than deep needs, draining dependency, and a refusal to accept responsibility for oneself.

Those who are fearful, distrustful, guilty, and dislike themselves cannot love—simply because they *cannot remove* the focus from themselves. They have not discovered their own identity and ego strength. Because they are uncomfortable with themselves, they are preoccupied with themselves and use vast amounts of psychic energy to protect their self images. In an oversimplified way, it's rather like the basketball player who notices that his shoelace is untied. His concentration is broken. He can't dribble, shoot, or fake; if someone steps on that shoelace, he will land on his nose on the hardwood floor. He is completely unable to turn his attention outward. Or, it is similar to the girl who, immediately upon entering a party, knows that she has erred—her dress is completely inappropriate for the occasion. She feels awkward, embarrassed, and self-conscious all evening. She can never loosen up and enjoy the party or the people, because her entire focus of attention is herself.

For many, love of self is a constant struggle throughout their lives. Insecure, certain that they have to fit a particular societal model, they teeter on the brink of agony, trying to be someone other than who they are. They often jeopardize their relationships by negatively questioning their worth and by selfishly looking for approbation from their partners. It becomes easier and easier to ignore the partner's needs, forget to restore his or her sense of self-worth, and neglect to nurture the growth of the relationship they mutually entered.

Interestingly, those who have not discovered their self-identity and self-worth go to great ends to protect their self-images. You know yourself that, no matter how angry you become with yourself, you never stop communicating with yourself. When you do something you classify as foolish, for example, you usually give yourself the benefit of any doubt. And, whatever problem confronts you, your first consideration is always, "how will this affect me?" The trick to loving yourself and, thus, to loving the other person is to say, "Self, move over. From now on he (or she) will be treated well, too!" In loving yourself and loving your partner as you love yourself, your love becomes creative. You and the one you love are created through your mutual caring.

LOVE IS CREATIVE

"Loving means summoning someone forth with the loudest most insistent call. Loving means stirring up in them a mute and hidden being who can't help leaping at the sound of your voice.

A being so new that even those who carried him within did not know him, yet so authentic that they can't fail to recognize him once they discover him.

All love includes fatherhood and motherhood. To love someone is to create him anew, to bid him to live, to invite him to grow."

Love creates the lover. If you "love" oranges and eat them regularly, you gain something—Vitamin C, strength, and energy. If you "love" a symphony and allow its sound to flow over you, the feelings it inspires become a part of you, and you become richer for the experience.

"When you love another person, you undergo the deepest transformation of all: reflected in the eyes of your beloved, you glimpse your ideal self."

From Susan, for example, Tom gets a vision of what she wants him to be, believes him to be, and what he might really be. With the security and inspiration of Susan's love, Tom dares to change, to strive to become his best self. He may put aside fears, become more sensitive, find the courage to take risks, and become motivated to use the talents he possesses. In pursuing the vision of himself revealed by Susan's love, Tom grows.

Love creates the beloved. Each partner brings certain strengths and weaknesses to the marriage. Married love should draw forth the best qualities in both. Susan knows, for example, that although Tom has seen the worst side of her personality on many occasions, he still loves her and wants her. Tom is able to feel the same about Susan. They know they have value, even with their weaknesses. They can be more secure and begin to drop their masks and defenses, because they don't need them anymore. They can get on with the business of being real. They can nurture their own inner strength and the strength of their marriage.

LOVE AND INNER STRENGTH

One of the great weaknesses of our society is that it primes us to be competitive without showing us how to be humble as well. Every one of us—man and woman, girl and boy—is encouraged to win the game, get top grades, be the most popular, close the deal, get ahead, and the "devil take the hindmost." Unfortunately, a couple can sometimes bring this competitive attitude to marriage, which often results in guardedness and the growth of unspoken envy and jealousy. One or both may then engage in "put downs" or try to make "brownie points" at the other's expense.

A touch of humility and some relearning may be required. Each of you should build up the other. Make him

43

or her a winner and you will be well on your way to having a rich, satisfying relationship. It takes humility to focus attention on someone other than yourself and to praise, cherish, and honor that person. A couple will usually have humility during the first throes of romantic love. But, when initial wonder and discovery fade and familiarity begins to dampen enthusiasm, you need virtue and inner strength to be constructive and humble in the relationship. Although this may be extremely obvious, it needs saying often and loudly. Any one of us can be weak and selfish; any one of us has the potential to hurt ourselves and anyone who gets within arm's length. This is particularly true in a close relationship. So without virtue, no marriage will make it.

Married love is built on truthfulness, patience, and a large measure of prudence, justice, temperance, and courage. It's also built on such things as consideration, manners, fair speech, and the ability to keep one's mouth shut and heart open as needed. The inner strength to make a marriage work should also give you the ability to give freely to your lover of your respect, yourself, and your possessions.

> "I love you
> Not only for what you are
> But for what I am
> When I am with you.
> I love you
> For putting your hand
> Into my heaped-up heart
> And passing over
> All the foolish, weak things
> That you cannot help but see there,
> And for drawing out into the light
> All of the beautiful qualities
> That no one else has ever looked
> Quite far enough to see."

LOVING IS BEING RESPECTFUL

"Respect" comes from two Latin words—"re," which means again, as in return or remake, and "spicere," which means "to look," as in the word spectator. Respect means to look again, to look more deeply, to perceive and appreciate the partner in his or her uniqueness.

You must respect the "otherness" of your partner and not bend, spindle, or manipulate him or her into a form you desire. Don't ever place your own limited vision of what your partner should be before the destiny to which God has called him.

Because Tom respects Susan, he will help her grow and unfold *in her own way,* to become the best possible person in her own right. If helping her grow and unfold means to encourage her to write, or sail, or skydive, etc., at the cost of time she might spend with him, Tom must still encourage her talent and her unique interests. Because Susan respects Tom, she will support his talents and interests, even if she prefers that nothing ever draw his interest away from her.

Respect means you don't expect your wife to pick the wet towel off the bathroom floor the way your mother did. *Look again,* she is not your mother. Respect means you don't expect your husband to treat you like a little girl and make everything right all of the time. *Look again,* he's not your father. *Respect means you always stand a little in awe before the* mystery of the person with whom you have chosen to spend your life.

LOVE IS GIVING

"It is better to give than to receive."

Why? Because giving is sometimes difficult, and because you suffer and feel noble? No! Because you experience the highest expression of your power as a person when you give yourself in love. You know that you are something and *have* something. Whether it be time, talent, counsel, tears, a word, an embrace, what you give in love is truly valuable simply because the other person needs and desires what you can give. When you give in love, you recognize yourself as valuable, worthwhile, and good.

A mother says, "When I was a child, *getting* the bicycle and dress were high points of my life. Now that I am more mature, *giving* the bicycles and dresses to my children and being responsible for and sharing their delight is much more rewarding than receiving something could ever possibly be."

"In giving, the beloved is enriched, too."

When you give in love, you enhance the other's sense of dignity and personal worth, because your love tells him or her that you consider him worthy of constant care and concern. Your love reinforces his value. When two people love each other in this fashion they rediscover themselves as individuals and discover together the beauty of their relationship. Love binds itself to and makes allowances for weaknesses in the person who is loved. Love sees and reinforces the best qualities in the beloved. Thus, lovers share a sense of aliveness to which they together have given birth.

LOVE IS THINKING

"Love is thinking, willing, and doing the good of another."

As rational beings, we can love in the fullest sense of the word because we can reason the good of another. As humans who love, as lovers and partners in marriage, you are constantly challenged to discern the partner's needs for growth and well-being. *This is the true norm of love in marriage ... discerning and promoting not what I want for the other, often not even what the beloved wants, but rather what he or she needs to become fully human.*

CASE A: "Peter G, computer designer—age 33." In eight years of marriage, Peter gave Martha a ranch house, a Jaguar, expensive jewelry, and trips to two international conferences. But he never gave her top place in his thoughts or in his heart's concern, because his career took priority. He gave her what he thought she ought to want. He loved her according to his thoughts and needs, not according to hers. Result: Separation.

LOVE IS WILLING

"Will, not the emotion, is the cornerstone of love."

Warm feelings of affection are ideal in marriage. But strained feelings do arise. Paul, for example, can be thoughtless sometimes; he can occasionally be cruel. Alice becomes despondent and rejecting. During these periods when affection is hidden, when feelings are hurt and hostility grows, *core love* must take over and stir the realization that, "I am committed to discover, to will, and to do the good of this person even if he or she is, for a time, thoroughly unlovable."

"...I do promise truly to love you even at those times, may they be few and far between, when you are most 'unlovable!'"

LOVING IS DOING

CASE B: "Margaret K, age 28." Margaret's husband John drinks more and more heavily. He claims it relaxes him when he's under pressure. For 15 months Margaret watches social drinking become alcoholic dependency, but does not confront John. Her norm of love is based on what her husband wants (to be left alone), not on what he needs—help. She knows what he needs. She wills it, too. But, when the time comes to do something about what he needs, it is just too painful.

As we said earlier in this chapter, true love requires strength. The Latin word for strength is "virtus;" the best marriages are made by people who are practiced and skilled in generosity, kindness, courage, patience, and honesty, among others.

Virtue is love in action. Strong love, faced with concrete situations of life that are often overwhelming or taxing, transmits the loving responses (virtues) of understanding, patience, compassion, and generosity.

THE OPPOSITE OF LOVE

Love is at once wondrous, joyful, fulfilling, challenging, and frighteningly fragile. Without constant nurturing and concern, the marital relationship can shatter.

The opposite of love, however, is not hatred; it is indifference. Love in marriage "ends not with a bang, but a whimper." Loss of love is almost always a slow process of erosion, boredom, taking each other for granted, and neglect, and of no longer investing time, attention, or imagination in each other.

Enthusiasm leaves first, then concern, and then caring. Then two people roam around, lost in the shell of an empty relationship. Soon someone else looks more attractive to them, and the end is near.

Keep alive! Keep growing as a person! Keep bringing your partner the gifts of new insights, deeper feelings,

MARRIAGE, THE SACRAMENT

LIKE THE EUCHARIST, marriage is
the giving and receiving of flesh and blood
for the life of the world,
a literal dying to self so that others may live abundantly.

LIKE BAPTISM, it is a birth into a greater communion,
a literal bestowal and revelation of life.

LIKE CONFIRMATION, it is a gradual growth
into mutual responsibility, a confirmation of
one another's being—body, soul, and spirit.

LIKE RECONCILIATION, marriage is a daily
practice and the school of forgiveness par excellence.

LIKE PRIESTHOOD, marriage becomes a ministry
of counsel and grace to another.

LIKE AN ANOINTING, as of the sick, it is a repeated
giving and receiving of healing touch.

MARRIAGE—here human flesh experiences
the wonder of divine love.
Here mutual rest becomes Sabbath refreshment,
conversation an entrance into the life of the Word,
and one another's company a presentiment
of the life of the Trinity.

—Patrick Jordan

© CHURCH magazine 2001. National Pastoral Life Center, Phone (212) 431-7825,
Fax (212) 274-9786; email syarri@nplc.org. Available in packs of 50.

enthusiasm, laughter, and interests.

"If your marriage is not daily being born it is dying."

"We are not born lovers. Love is a task, a skill, an art we must work at until the day we die!"

"Love is an activity, not a passion.
Its essence is to 'labor' for someone
To make someone grow.
To love a person productively implies
To care and feel responsible
For the development of all his human powers."

The second hardest thing in all the world is to engage
in the trying process of living intimately with one other person.
The hardest thing in all the world is living alone.

BUILDING RELATIONSHIP

Building a strong, caring relationship is often a slow, painful process that might be likened to two porcupines approaching each other for warmth. If they remain far apart, they stay cold. If they come too close together, they prick one another. In the human relationship, finding just the right distance for greatest warmth and intimacy without intruding upon or hurting the other takes learning. Testing and fielding one another is important to the process of adjustment.

THE INFLUENCE OF YOUR PAST

All of us interpret reality to suit our own views. As one prominent psychologist put it, "We all peep out at the world through our own separate knotholes. We see everything through the unique lens of our own mindset."

You and your fiance have been conditioned by approximately twenty years of experiences that might be very similar or very different. Whether from similar or different experiences and backgrounds, however, your family, friends, school, work life, etc., have helped mold you in a very distinctive way. You have different strong points and weaknesses, different levels of confidence, different defense mechanisms. You have convictions, preferences, and prejudices that may differ. Your patterns of learning, decision-making, and problem-solving vary, and even your lifestyles may be quite different.

The worst possible mistake you can make is to assume that your partner will share all or even most of your attitudes, ideas, reactions, or behavior patterns. However, during dating and courtship, understanding begins to grow, and some of the differences between you begin to be resolved or accepted.

THE INFLUENCE OF COURTSHIP

During courtship, you discovered and responded to attractive qualities in each other—her liveliness, the way she laughed or could put people at ease; or, his seriousness and drive or crazy imagination. You found many common interests: you like the same restaurants; enjoy the same TV shows; grow angry about the same issues; hate or love country-western music. As time passed, you compared temperaments, ideas, and life goals, and you found that they fit with each other rather well. Ultimately, you found that you filled each other's psychological and physical needs enough to say, "Let's get married."

. During courtship, both partners are on their "best behavior" most of the time. Like the salesman who tries to impress a customer, you both take pains to hide faults and flaws and to protect your image. New love, with the heady discovery of being wanted, the excitement born of nearness, and the promise of sexual involvement turns the lover's gaze away from any problems or potential problem areas. New love can lead couples to discount or minimize negative traits and danger signals. Each has a tendency to say, "Oh, he'll give that up," or "She isn't really like that," and focus exclusively on the good qualities. As the saying goes, love is blind.

Although courtship provided you the opportunity to learn many things about your partner, you had only limited opportunities to see him or her in typical life situations or to discover how he or she might behave in a crisis or when faced with boredom or conflict. You had limited opportunities to see his temper when he is tired or irritated or her tendency to withdraw when she is hurt or confused.

When you enter marriage, therefore, bringing many differences, some similarities, and a host of expectations, you begin a process of adjustment that will continue throughout your marriage.

THE PROCESS OF MARITAL ADJUSTMENT

Adjustment means negotiating and arranging factors in a situation so that each party is treated fairly; so that the needs and wishes of each are met, insofar as possible, and so that greater satisfaction results for all. In marriage, adjustment means doing that which is appropriate or necessary for the satisfaction and growth of both parties and of the relationship. Marriage is a fitting together of personalities, skills, and preferences on every level—from sharing deep emotions to sharing household responsibilities and chores.

Adjustment in marriage requires two equal, fairly well-matched players. Don't let it become a game of solitaire in which "the two shall be one, and I'll be the one!" Successful marital adustment is not mere role-playing, a studied pretext to avoid mutuality and conceal from others the lack of a true partnership. Such pretext often masks the perennial human desire to dominate and control the relationship through subtle manipulation.

Adjustment is not submission. If one partner is afraid to express himself (herself) or make demands, or desires peace at any price, he or she can cause the relationship to become sour because of their frustrations. Neither is adjusting; instead, they are disappearing as persons. Adjustment is not putting together a relationship that is only tolerable, like in a cold war. Adjustment is a creative process that requires full willingness to promote the potential of the partner and the relationship.

Adjustment and Decision-Making. In a sense, the decisions you reach are not as important as the process. The more deeply and honestly you analyze and discuss a matter, the more constructive the decisions that you reach. When both of you have participated in the decision-making process, you will be more willing to live with the conclusions.

What if a significant situation arises that produces clear-cut disagreement? You want to change jobs and move to another town. Your partner does not want to move so far away from family and friends and may also have a good job already. If, after reasoned discussion, things still come out pretty even, then both must consider who has most at stake and what will have the most positive impact on the relationship. Because a majority vote is not possible when only two are casting ballots, someone has to compromise, moving toward the other to say, "Okay, we'll take a flyer and go," or, "Oh, let's forget about it for now and see what happens." If true, honest dialogue has occurred, either decision is likely to become more acceptable to both partners.

When the moment of truth comes in any decision, there is the temptation to dig in and stand firm. One of you might say to yourself, "The reasons sound more sensible all the time, but if I keep saying no, she'll give in." Mistake! If one option begins to look better, move toward it and feel your way into it. Remember, the object of dialogue is a wise decision and good adjustment—not winning. Every time someone wins, someone loses, and after a while losers can get bitter. Moreover, the one who compromises should do so as wholeheartedly and enthusiastically as possible. You are a team. Once the play is called, you should both exert yourselves to make it work. Don't lie back in the grass, waiting for the chance to shout. "I told you so!" Finally, the one whose viewpoint prevails, must be especially supportive and ready to help with the partner's areas of concern.

Let's see what the adjustment process might look like in one area of decision-making, that is, what ties will you maintain with both sets of in-laws?

First, consider the real issues and goals involved. View them as objectively as possible.

- Our relatives would like us to visit frequently.
- We want to keep in contact. We have positive feelings toward them, although some trouble spots do exist.
- We don't want to get smothered, or trapped into visiting patterns that they will want us to maintain for years.

Analyze how you truly feel about the issues.
- I don't really mind going to her parents' house. The food is good, but it gets boring after a couple of hours.

- My family is gone. It's nice to be part of hers.
- If I go along with her, she owes me something.
- His family is fine, but when his mother gets critical, I get angry. He doesn't seem to notice.

Share your feelings! How do your feelings fit your basic goals?

- We respect our parents and want to maintain a good relationship. Besides, they lent us money and we are grateful. Also, children need grandparents.
- Tom's mother is overly possessive and he ought to loosen that tie. It prevents him from functioning as maturely as he can.

Consider which of you has the most at stake in the decision.

- Sarah is the only daughter of a doting father and mother.
- Tom is one of nine children. His parents hardly remember his name.

Consider who must live with the decision and who will suffer the major consequences.

- If we don't visit regularly, Sarah will get a lot of flak from her mother.

How do your friends, relatives, or people you admire solve similar problems? Does their approach hold any clues for you?

Having considered and discussed these factors, try to draw some conclusions and set up some guidelines that are agreeable to both of you.

- We'll try to keep a flexible schedule of visits.
- We'll try to *do* things with our parents rather than sit around searching for conversation.
- We'll see them more.
- We'll see them less.
- We'll make no major commitments in this area without checking with each other.

56

Adjustment and Personal Habits. Scores of areas, from the trivial to the vitally important, require adjustment. A list of a few areas is provided to stimulate discussion.

- *Appearance*— Will his underwear–and–bare feet approach at home offend you? Will your wearing curlers turn him off? Will you expect him to shave on a day off? Will you allow her to select your clothes?

- *Privacy*—Do you need time by yourself to think, to reflect, and to putter? How do you tell your partner without seeming to reject him or her?

- *Social Life*—You want a minimum of four nights a month out with your friends; she says, "We married to be together." What do you say?

- *Entertainment*—"One Life to Loaf" is your favorite program; she can't stand it. Do you adjust or does it become an issue?

- *Housekeeping*—How clean is clean? How neat is neat? Where do you draw the line between informal, lived-in, and sloppy?

- *Rhythm*—You are a morning person (there are a few!) who leaps out of bed and starts the day with a brisk five-mile run. You wind down at sunset, but she can go on for half the night. You're a charger. She likes to savor things.

- *Ritual*—For you, things should be done with style and grace; meals are an occasion. He'd rather eat informally; food is fuel.

Adjustment and Societal Roles. Until recently, marriage in our society was a male dominated affair. "That's the way things were meant to be," they said. The husband was head of the household, made decisions, gave commands, and ran the show (at least, that was the image). The wife's role was to honor, obey, and not make waves. She was

57

totally dependent on her husband economically and couldn't do much, even if she tried. Today, husbands and wives are encouraged to be equal partners. The concept seems so new, however, that we have no tradition that teaches people how to live with one another as equals in mutual respect and trust. And even the best intentions cannot stop you from imitating more traditional behavior and patterns of relating that you witnessed in your own parents.

Men, in their attitudes toward women, can range from typically chauvinistic to completely understanding and supportive. And women, in their attitudes, can run the spectrum from the highly traditional to the extreme feminist. Even if the concept does not seem particularly important to you now, you should explore how each of you feels about the changing roles of men and women. Your attitudes will have an impact on your careers, decision-making, control of money, independence, outside activities, and your lifestyle in general.

Adjustment in Early Marriage. The first weeks and months of early marriage can sometimes be a "trial and error" testing ground during which a couple, often with different backgrounds, and certainly with different behavioral patterns, tries to establish compatible lifestyles and mesh lives and habits together. For some couples, this early period can be quite stressful—a circumstance that they could not have anticipated during the exciting months before the wedding day and honeymoon.

The honeymoon is "time away," usually spent travelling to new and intriguing places. Leisure time, recreational activities, and the excitement of the sexual relationship make the experience a delightful one, although one which gives a couple little preparation for the realities of making a life together. Returning from the honeymoon to their new apartment, the anticipation that preceded the wedding and honeymoon over and excitement tempered, a newly married couple might experience quite a letdown. Immediate surroundings might be new and perhaps forbidding. Familiar surroundings and family no longer provide reassurance.

At the same time, newlyweds are thrust into an intimate, living together situation with partners for whom they truly care and are anxious to please, but who, on many levels, are still strangers. Continual closeness takes some adjustment, and learning to adapt to the other's habits and idiosyncracies without impatience or conflict is no small task.

Some of the longstanding habits that can cause tension and even conflict in the early days of marriage include eating habits; sleeping routines; TV watching; personal rituals having to do with cleanliness, dressing, and comfort; housekeeping; socializing; reading; sexual signaling; and homemaking roles.

For example:

- He thinks entertaining is dip, chips, and beer. She thinks it's an elegant dinner.
- She prefers a skimpy breakfast. He likes a hearty one.
- To her, saving is having a formal bank account. To him, it's tucking money away in a book.
- For him, television may be a constant companion. For her, it's a resource for special programs.
- For her, music requires close attention. For him, it should be played quietly in the background.
- To her, cleaning is dusting and straightening up. For him, it's a major overhaul.
- To him, bathing is a brief necessity. For her, it's a time for relaxation.

- For him, bedtime is at 10:45 PM. For her, it's 12:45 PM.

Questionable habits (like flicking cigarette ashes on the floor or leaving a pile of dirty clothes on the bathroom floor) can be magnified if neither partner tries to understand how the other feels about it. In a marriage between an excessively neat person and one who is not at all meticulous, watch out for the "Odd Couple Syndrome." Unless you can work out a compromise, conflict over differing habits might be irresolvable.

Simply sleeping in the same bed with someone might be difficult at first. And, if that someone snores, grinds his or her teeth, grabs all the blankets, or tosses and kicks while asleep, it might be unnerving until you both adjust. Sometimes the Odd Couple Syndrome might be noticed in differences in morning habits: One of you might leap up instantly alert, good humored, and ready to discuss the day's events, while the other is a zombie until after the second cup of coffee. On the other hand, one of you might be a night owl, able to stay up late watching TV or reading, while the other—who requires more sleep or has to get up earlier in the morning—cannot. Neither should try to force the other to adjust to his or her schedule; both should try to work out a compatible schedule based on each other's individual needs.

PRIVACY AND YOUR OWN "SPACE"

The need for one's own "space," for time to oneself, and for occasional moments of solitude is perhaps greater in a close relationship than at any other time. The constant presence of the one you love is at once exciting and potentially suffocating. The physical sharing of the same limited space can cause stress throughout marriage if each of you does not make an effort to respect the other's need to be alone at times, to work on a project without interruption, or to be silent and contemplative once in awhile. Learn to recognize these needs early in marriage and both of you will cherish time spent together.

Although all of us need attention and activity, we also need quiet moments. Each of you has to learn to interpret the signals that indicate the other's need for moments alone. If that need happens to come at a time when *you* need attention, you may have to wait for that attention. Try to avoid the temptation to intrude on the other's quiet time; especially try not to lure your partner into activity with you. Frustrated by the interruption, your partner will give his or her attention begrudgingly.

TALKING IT OUT

Differences in personalities, interests, and habits are the spice and zest of a relationship. In the early months and years of marriage, these differences might appear to be insurmountable—if you don't talk about them with one another. Usually, none of them are terribly important in and of themselves; but, the cumulative impact of all real and perceived problems can be devastating if you harbor negative thoughts about them. It is important to talk about them, laugh about them, and try to work them out together.

Tense, rigid, or anxious people can explode in anger or quake in fear when the eggs are hard-boiled rather than soft-boiled or when a dish is dropped and shattered. Such trivial problems will hardly break a relationship, but if their occurrence generates unease or hostility, it could be symptomatic of a deeper inability to communicate, seek understanding, or make an effort to please and work out constructive solutions.

61

The response each partner has to the other (rigid and stubborn or kind and generous); the positions each assumes in the interplay (punishing or punished; demanding or cooperative; manipulative or compromising); and the amount of creativity and honest communication brought to bear on problem-solving can imprint and establish positive or negative behavior patterns for a long time to come.

THE REWARDS OF RELATIONSHIP AND ADJUSTMENT

As you confront life's situations together and take the time to listen, communicate your needs, and adjust to your partner's needs, your marriage will be a complex mosaic of potential grandeur that you can create piece by piece, experience by experience, and decision by decision. Creating the mosaic requires compatibility (personality fit), mutual agreement, and mutual satisfaction. Because the marriage relationship is unique and highly personal, one couple's approach is not necessarily right and another's wrong

"What is real?" asked the rabbit one day when they were lying side by side. "Does it mean having things that buzz inside you, and a stickout handle?" "Real isn't how you're made," said the skin-horse, "it's a thing that happens to you. When a child loves you for a long, long time —not just to play with—but really loves you, then you become real." "Does it hurt?" asked the rabbit. "Sometimes," said the skin-horse— for he always was truthful. "When you are real, you don't mind being hurt." "Does it happen all at once like being wound up, or bit by bit?" "It doesn't happen all at once. You become. It takes a long time. That's why it doesn't often happen to people who break easily, or have sharp edges, or have to be carefully kept. Generally, by the time you are real most of your hair has been loved off and your eyes drop out and you get loose at the joints and very shabby. But these things don't matter at all. Because once you are real, you can't be ugly, except to people who don't understand."

M. Williams

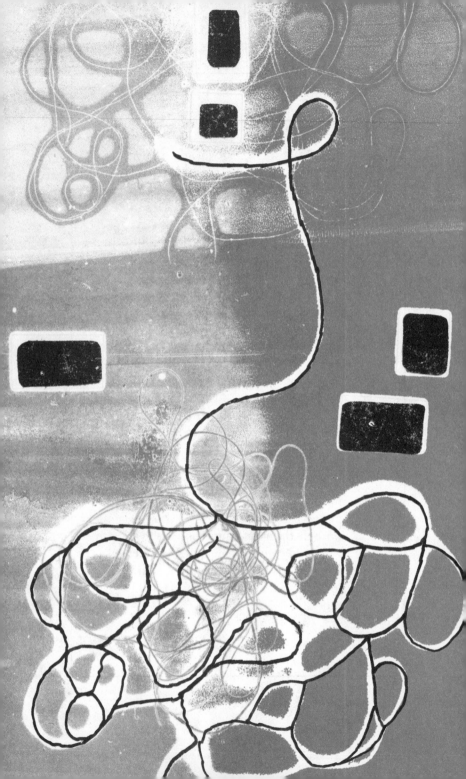

Communication

Dialogue in marriage is as vital to the growth of the relationship as circulation of the blood is to continued physical health. Blood brings nourishment and clean air and carries away poisons and wastes. If circulation is impaired, the body sickens and may die. Dialogue brings new ideas and signs of caring and acceptance, and it carries away fears and anxieties. If dialogue is impaired, the relationship weakens and may die.

Many couples continue to grow in intimacy and thoughtful communication long after the first outburst of loving communication during courtship and early marriage. Others, who become fearful as protective masks and disguises are stripped away, begin to hold back. They limit communication to certain "safe" areas. Rather than discuss how they feel and who they are, they talk about the weather, television, and the price of things. They begin a slow descent into boredom and mutual irritation.

THE MEANING OF WORDS

One of the chief deterrants to good communication is the *special meaning* that people have for certain words, ideas, and events. They assume that the partner applies the same meaning as well. However, we each have our own unique reactions and interpretations.

Example. Tom, unwinding after a difficult day, stretches out on the couch. Ann leans down to kiss him. "Hey," he sighs, "I really need to be waited on and babied tonight." Ann stiffens and quickly leaves to go set the table. Puzzled, Tom realizes that her abrupt withdrawal must have been caused by something he said. After some gentle probing, they discover, to Ann's surprise, that the word, "baby" triggered her negative reaction: It carried emotions from earliest childhood. To be a baby meant to be weak, helpless, and dependent. "Don't be a baby," was her mother's constant injunction. When her husband asks to be treated like a baby, she is visibly upset.

THE MEANING OF FEELINGS

How do you enter into your partner's world of meanings and feelings? Simply by trying to pay attention, by learning to listen with the "third ear" of sensitivity for changes in mood or feeling. If your partner should suddenly stop talking, look hurt, or react with undue anger, stop the conversation right there! What is happening *between you* at that moment is far more important than the subject you are discussing. If you can't sense the cause of the change, you might say, "Listen, something I said caused you a problem. Can we talk about it and work our way through it?" Any potential problem can thus be defused.

The skill of tracking and entering the feelings of the other is called "empathy," i.e., putting yourself into your partner's "frame of reference," trying to see and feel the situation as he or she does. Before you can develop empathy, you need to have insight, and you need to understand your own feelings.

Some people go through life never having been in touch with their own feelings. They have a fuzzy, general awareness of their emotions, and they rarely reflect on them. If asked, "How do you feel?" they usually say, "I feel fine" or "I feel miserable." Such people often see no patterns, no cause or effect in their emotional lives.

Example. Joan receives an unexpected compliment and is elated for hours, but never relates the mood to the compliment. Tom has a major bill to pay at the end of the week and is really worried. Throughout the week he is surly and snappish, but never realizes that his fears about debt have triggered these reactions. *If we recognize our feelings, we can work with them.*

Example. On his way home one evening after losing a sale and being criticized by his boss, Dan realizes he is depressed and irritable. If he says to Maryanne, "Hey, I'm not feeling well, I'm pretty edgy, and I need some quiet time," things could go very smoothly. If, on the other hand, he is not in touch with his feelings, he may release angry emotions at his wife or children without ever realizing why.

The person with poor self-insight has difficulty empathizing with others; we use our experience of self to help us recognize the feelings of others.

Example. Bob comes home late; Zelda is very uptight. He could immediately interpret this as an unreasonable response to his being late, or he could try to discover the cause of her feelings. A myriad of factors other than his tardiness might be at the root of her anger or irritation. Perhaps she's irritated at a phone call from her mother, or perhaps the children have been uncontrollable. More than likely, she was frightened that something had happened to him. Discovering the cause of these feelings helps a couple deal with problems, not just with symptoms.

THE MEANING OF ACCEPTANCE

Warm, nonjudgmental acceptance is the most important factor in good communication.

Some people stimulate and reassure us. In their presence, we speak easily and freely. We sense that they respect us and care about what we are saying. We are comfortable with them and reveal our ideas and some of our deeper feelings. Other people shut us off; they threaten us and cause fear—the greatest deterrant to good communication. In their presence, we become uncommunicative and reveal nothing. They seem to say, "You are too insignificant to command my attention," or they seem ready to criticize. With them, we become defensive and protective.

Example. A frightened little boy, having broken a window, says, "Don't tell my mother, I'll pay for it." His mother is the most important person in his life and her *good opinion* is tremendously important.

To each other, marriage partners are special, valued persons. They value each other's opinion, and neither wants the other to see his or her faults and weaknesses. Two people in love become very important to each other and quite vulnerable; they can hurt each other very deeply. They are often tempted to hide anything that could potentially harm their partner's image of them, unless they can trust the partner to understand.

Trying to express deep feelings is like swimming in the early Spring. You test the water carefully, wading in slowly and gingerly. If it's too cold, you withdraw. Likewise, we often test for the warmth and coldness of another person's response. For example, Al tells Jan he's unhappy with his job. How do you rate these answers?

a) "You certainly shouldn't be satisfied; they're not pay- you much."
b) "Oh, I'm not terribly happy with the things I have to do either."
c) "Don't start that! We've too many bills to pay for you to think about changing jobs."
d) "We all get discouraged. What do you want for sup- per?"
e) "You sound really upset. Tell me a little more."

Of all, only "e" invites further communication.

- Maryanne tells Dan, "A young man came by selling magazines and..." Dan breaks in, "Don't tell me you were taken in by some door-to-door con man!"

Maryanne immediately sees Dan as Lord High Execu- tioner and may lie about the magazines she bought. Next time it will be harder to talk with him.

- Bob drinks too much and is loud at a party. On the way home, Zelda says, "You are a drunken exhibi- tionist!"

Bob is sullen, apologizes, or strikes back. Or, Zelda can express her feelings, "I was kind of embarrassed." Bob might then respond, "Why?" and communication can pro- ceed. A problem was confronted without accusations.

Accusation destroys acceptance. Sometimes an attack can be seen in the words themselves. "You louse!" Some- times an attack is felt in the tone of voice used. From tender and endearing to downright vicious, the following statement can be said and heard in a variety of ways: *"I just love it when you do that!"*

Certain phrases sometimes carry hidden accusations that invite hostile responses. For example:

- "What's wrong with you now?" (There is always something wrong with you. What is it this time?)

- "This is more than I can expect from you, but…" (You have proven incapable of doing reasonable, constructive things, but I'll give you a chance even though I know you'll fail.)

- "How many times do I have to ask you…" (You are trying on purpose to frustrate my plans.)

How do you interpret the following phrases:

- "Didn't you promise me that you would…"
- "What's the use of reminding you…"
- "Where did you ever get the idea…"
- "I don't want to complain, but…"

NONVERBAL COMMUNICATION

Language is developed much later than expressive movements of face or body, which go back almost to the beginning of man's evolution. The body does speak; it weeps with *joy*, shakes with *rage*, tenses muscles in *apprehension*, or relaxes muscles in *contentment*. Our eyes alone can be piercing, flashing, cold, hooded, twinkling, leering, smoldering, or blank and lifeless.

Books on body language have tried to ascribe very specific meanings to every gesture and movement. Although some critics claim that these interpretations are carried too far, nonverbal communication does exist, and it is very important in marriage. Partners learn to recognize scores of expressions, reactions, and signals that pass between them which are perceived by no one else.

Gestures, posture, and facial expressions are often spontaneous and quick, and they tend to send more honest messages than the words we superimpose on them. We have all learned to be careful about what we say—to please people, to fit in, to hide our feelings—but we haven't learned to control all the signals our body sends. After a quarrel, one partner says, calmly, "All right, let's do it your way." His words are concilliatory, but his rigid body and his clenched fist and set jaw shout defiance.

TOUCH

> "Touch is one of the most expressive
> forms of human communication."

In our culture, especially in those regions influenced by Puritan heritage, touch is considered suspect, and some couples might have to overcome an upbringing in which they were taught never to touch. They have to learn—or relearn—the value of a caress, a protective arm around the shoulder, and the joys of nuzzling and cuddling that bespeak care, affection, and concern. Touch is an important aspect of communication that brings us joyously and warmly together. To relegate touch in marriage to moments of sexual contact only can deprive you of the joy of communicating other than through speech alone.

TIMING

The mood and setting for dialogue can sometimes determine whether you communicate with or irritate one another. Stress, fatigue, different expectations, tension, the common cold, alcohol, etc., can all affect the ability to communicate clearly and lovingly. Problems can usually be avoided, or discussed rationally, when both partners feel good. Taking time to care, to listen, to pay attention to one another, is important. If work, family, children, or social commitments begin to infringe upon your time together to keep you from fulfilling the need to talk, look at ways in which you can relieve those pressures and steal some moments together. You might do something as unheard of as taking a walk. Or, an occasional weekend away might be beneficial. *Finding time to talk together*—whether it be a half-hour before bedtime or Sunday morning after breakfast—*is not easy*. Make a commitment to take the time.

THE SILENT TREATMENT

The "silent treatment"—when one partner chooses to completely ignore the other and allow no communication —can be overwhelming. You can feel hurt, angry, frustrated, frightened, or vengeful. The silence contains a message that can create intense reactions. It appears to mean complete rejection. A person given the silent treatment can only turn inward or try to force his way through the barrier by increased shouting, or perhaps violence. Each partner has to look at his or her own feelings and those of the partner, keeping in mind the drastic effect that the unwarranted "cold shoulder" can have on future communication in the relationship.

On the other hand, silence can be "golden." Withdrawal from certain discussions can be constructive at times. If you're involved in a prolonged discussion that is causing irritation and wearing you both down with useless repetition, you might say, "Look, let's step back and take a new perspective on the problem." Gather your resources, for caring is vital to continued good communication.

When you argue, don't dig up the past. One of the great temptations we face when losing a quarrel is to seek more ammunition from the great storehouse of remembered faults and foibles. "What about the time you promised to come straight home from the office party and never made it until dawn?" Keep things current. Talk about how you feel *now*.

Be careful not to use certain words and phrases that you know can hurt the other. "You're a coward!" "You're frigid!" "I don't know what I ever saw in you!" These are some "atomic" phrases that can blow up a relationship. Once spoken, although regretted instantly, these words are poisoned arrows flying toward the target, never to be recalled.

GUNNY-SACKING

Susan gets home from work forty-five minutes late. George "blows his top," reacting in anger out of proportion to her "offense." Why? Because George has been gunny-sacking. He has collected a series of complaints about Susan over the past several months, but has suppressed his irritation—perhaps because he hates unpleasant scenes or sees himself as strong and noble, able to bear everything.

Each time he experienced a negative feeling toward Susan, George stuffed it into his psychic gunny-sack and dragged it with him for day to day. This latest incident causes the sack to burst open. Both of them become engulfed in a messy situation, and Susan is swamped in a whirlpool of George's aggressions. She is confused, threatened, and soon angry.

When you have an honest concern, talk about it. Clear it up while it is still minor. Occasional confrontations, even if accompanied by some friction, can be growthful situations that lead to understanding, and they are certainly preferable to an artificial calm that hides honest feelings.

NAGGING

To nag is "to annoy by continual fault-finding, scolding, complaining, and urging." Nagging *does not work*. After the sixth week of badgering your partner about sewing on some buttons, it should be clear that she does not see the problem the way you do, particularly after such persistent requests.

Nagging involves criticism and implies inadequacy, bad will, or irresponsibility. It is not unusual that nagging be met with impatience, anger, or frustration. Look deeper; track the feelings. Find out *why* the problem is there and how it can be overcome or avoided.

A NOTE ON MARRIAGE COUNSELING

If you should develop serious misunderstandings and cannot handle some of the situations that confront you, you may need to talk with an outsider. If so, choose a wise, mature person or seek qualified, professional help. Do this *before* the situation becomes irreparable. Guidance from an objective third party is often all that's needed to help you find your way back to each other.

"Communication is the art of sharing ideas, feelings, and expressions. In marriage, it is the skill of expressing and receiving insights and emotions in such a way that greater understanding and acceptance result. With good communication, disagreements are minimized, differences recognized and respected, expectations blended, and common courses of action taken."

Sexuality is a complex attribute of every person, involving his deepest needs for identity, relationship, love and immortality.

Sexuality and Sensuality

"The most serious danger to a true sexual renaissance in our time comes from the culture's alienation of sex from love, emotions, and commitment. But the resiliency and good sense of mankind may yet prevail. Along with eroticism, the ideals of romance, meaning, fidelity, and love are staging a comeback. Tender concern and responsibility could flourish; the playboy may yet become a man; and the playmate a valiant woman."

Sexuality is a quality of personality; the strong power and potential of sexuality is part of "self." Sex is not only something you do; sex is something *you are.* Sex is mind and body, spirit and emotion. You are a sexual being, and sex and sexuality are you. Love, value, feelings, trust, responsibility—yes, and even fear, pain, and heartbreak are all part of you as a sexual human being; all are necessary to render sexuality human. God created human sexuality. It is His gift, and it is good.

Sex is within us, and we, as sexual persons, determine what it will mean, what it will do, and what we can do with sex. Sexuality is one of the most important powers and attributes every person has. Because of our sexuality, we have the potential to create love or to destroy it. When fit into a larger framework of human meaning and shaped to serve man's noblest values and deepest needs—such as personal growth, true intimacy, committed love, marriage and family—sexuality is responsible. If, however, sexuality is given different meanings, made an end unto itself, used selfishly, exploitatively, or without regard to consequences, sexuality is irresponsible.

CONFRONTING YOUR SEXUALITY

Every person has an idea of and ideal for himself or herself. From our culture, we each hold an image—clear or confused—of what we could be: generous, noble, wise, responsible, dedicated, even heroic. Along with this image, we have our knowledge of and experience with sex. We know sex has the power to rivet and compel our attention and make us forget everything else. Its urge toward pleasure can make us try to attract, possess, or even use another person. We realize that a preoccupation with or misuse of sexuality can and does lead to loss of self-ideal; we could fall short of what we can be and cause ourselves shame.

Sex can lead a person to neglect work or career, deceive himself and others, exploit people, act selfishly, forget responsibilities, leave wife or husband and family, break commitments, etc. Used unwisely, sex has the potential for harming self and others and can lead us to sin. Like the use of a gun, car, liquor, or money, the use of sex has a moral dimension. But, unlike guns, cars, liquor, or money, which are external objects that we can enjoy, abuse, or *simply ignore*, sex is part of us and cannot be ignored. Sexuality and sexual desires must be confronted, channeled responsibly, and used to extend and enhance our values. Used wisely, sexuality aids and abets our growth and maturity.

THE DIMENSIONS OF SEXUALITY

Your physiological maleness or femaleness and your body shape and organs were determined at the moment you were conceived. Before birth you carried egg cells (as a female) or the beginning of sperm cells (as a male). Today, every one of the three billion cells in your body is clearly male or female. Your "package" of sexual traits (gender) is a biochemical given on which your personality and development are based.

From the moment of birth you are taught a role that is based on your sex. Your parents' attitudes, the toys and clothes you were given, the chores you were asked to do, and the games you were "supposed to" play all taught you accepted behavior patterns for males and females in our society. Your perceptions of the world are based on your development as male or female, and the world's perception of you is based on your role as a male or female.

Sexuality is universal, however. Other dimensions of sexuality—like psychological dynamism; physical and psychological pleasure; ambiguity; and the complexity of expressive, communicative, and procreative aspects of sex—are derived from our deep needs to love and to express ourselves through love. They are derived from the unique physical and psychological responses of males and females.

For example, psychological dynamism (some refer to it as "chemistry") is a mysterious, inexplicable emotional current that flows continuously between males and females. Dynamism is awareness, interest, attraction, excitement, deep desire, or the need only to be noticed and appreciated by members of the opposite sex. Sometimes the chemistry is low key and imperceptible. At other times, like during infatuation or first love, this dynamism can be surprisingly intense. This chemistry will be a wonderful aspect of your interpersonal relationships until death.

Closely related to dynamism are the intense physical and psychological excitement and pleasure produced by sexual arousal and involvement. From the early teens, we are aware that the opposite sex can cause bodily stirrings and tensions within us. We know almost instinctively that "this isn't all there is," that reactions become more intense and far deeper as sexual involvement becomes more intimate.

Sexual attraction and desire are strong factors that interest two people in one another and lead them to begin a relationship. Shared sexual pleasure can facilitate the growth of a rich, deep relationship. In a human and Christian sense, sexual relations should be preceded by getting to know one another and building trust, caring, and love, which lead to commitment and taking responsibility for each other. Sex is uniquely designed for and carries the potential of fostering the deepest of interpersonal relationships—marriage.

Because human beings are complex and have a broad range of emotions and needs, sexuality and the expression of sexuality are complex. Sexual activity, therefore, can be playful, solemn, passionate, joyful, exciting, or matter-of-fact. It can be used to console, encourage, thank, communicate, give and share pleasure, and express love.

Sexual activity can also be used selfishly—to dominate, bargain, punish, insult, or exploit. Just as our emotions are often ambiguous, sexual activity—a touch, a kiss, an embrace, the act of intercourse itself—can often carry ambiguous meaning. In sexual relations, if intercourse is to be love-making, people must put love into it. Because it involves the total person, sexual activity can be a powerful, symbolic language. It can carry deep messages: "I need you. I'm sorry. I forgive you. I love you." These words can easily be spoken between two people. When they are confirmed in the marriage bed, however, they are far more compelling, convincing, and satisfying.

Sex also has the potential to be procreative: Fully human sexuality involves the possibility of new life. The design of our sexual organs, the physiology of reproduction, and the powerful psychology of arousal, all stimulate the couple to union. This endows the art of intercourse with great responsibility and tell us that one of the primary reasons for union between a man and a woman is parenthood and continuing the human race.

THE PHYSIOLOGY OF REPRODUCTION

The Female Reproductive System. A young girl begins puberty at about 11 or 12, when the pituitary gland in the brain secretes hormones that cause a period of rapid growth and important changes in the reproductive system. The changes occur in the ovaries and the uterus and cause the cyclical event of menstruation.

Ovaries. The ovaries are two organs located on either side of the abdominal cavity, about six inches below the waist. They contain thousands of microscopic egg cells that have been present in the woman's body since before she was born. Each egg cell contains chromosomes and genes that mingle with the chromosomes of the male sperm cell at conception to give a child its unique genetic code and inherited characteristics. Beginning at puberty, ovulation occurs on a regular basis, usually every 28 days. Each ovary, on an alternating basis, brings an egg cell to maturity and releases it into the fallopian tube. (This monthly process will usually continue for at least thirty years.) During a period of several days, the egg travels through the fallopian tube on its way to the uterus, or womb. If fertilization of the egg is to occur, it will almost always happen in the fallopian tube.

The uterus is shaped like a pear and has an open, narrow lower end. The uterus is composed of strong, elastic muscle tissue that can stretch during pregnancy. Every month when the egg is released from the ovary, hormones stimulate the uterus to prepare itself to receive and nourish a fertilized egg. The uterus develops a thick, soft, spongy lining. Upon arrival in the uterus, a fertilized egg embeds itself in the uterine lining. The newly conceived embryo develops during nine months of pregnancy in this highly protected environment, nourished by the mother's blood.

The Vagina. The lower end of the uterus is connected to a passage called the vagina. The vagina is the opening that receives the penis during intercourse. The vagina is capable of great expansion, for it is also the birth canal. The opening is covered by two folds of flesh called labia. At the top of the labia is a tiny organ called the clitoris, which contains numerous nerve endings sensitive to stimulation.

The Hymen. The vaginal passage is partially covered by a very thin membrane called the hymen. An open hymen is no indication of lack of virginity; young women who engage in a great deal of physical activity usually stretch and open the hymen long before marriage. If, however, the hymen is still intact at marriage, it will be stretched and opened during initial sexual relations. The woman will feel pressure when the penis is inserted into the vagina, and, as the membrane stretches, minor discomfort and slight bleeding might occur. Only in the most rare cases is the membrane so thick that sexual intercourse is difficult or painful. In such instances, a physician should be consulted.

More than 99 per cent of the time, the egg cell is not fertilized and simply dissolves in the bodily fluids. The soft lining of the uterus and the blood supply it contains also dissolve shortly after ovulation and are disposed of as menstrual flow. Ovulation and menstruation do not occur during pregnancy, because secretion of the special hormones regulating these processes is suspended as soon as fertilization of the egg takes place.

THE MALE REPRODUCTIVE SYSTEM

A boy enters puberty at about 12 or 13, at which time the testicles and penis reach maturity. The testicles produce sperm and are contained in the scrotum, a soft, fleshy pouch at the base of the penile shaft. The testicles begin to manufacture sperm during puberty. Billions of sperm are produced, and each sperm cell has an oval-shaped head (nucleus) and a tail which enables it to swim through bodily fluids.

The penis is a fleshy, tubular organ which is soft and retracted when not aroused. The tip of the penis, called the glans, is rich in nerve endings that become highly sensitive to contact when erection occurs.

THE PHYSIOLOGY OF SEX

Sexual Arousal. Genital sexual arousal is somewhat similar in males and females. The penis, the clitoris, and the labia contain spongelike erectile tissue. When sexual arousal occurs, blood is pumped forcefully and "locked" into the erectile tissue, causing the tissue to become extended and swollen (tumescent). Penile erection occurs in the male and clitoral erection in the female. The clitoris is one of the most important centers of sexual arousal in the woman's body. Gentle manual manipulation of the clitoris and labia during foreplay normally serves to heighten the woman's state of arousal and intensify her desire for penetration.

As sexual arousal increases, the labia become more firm and open wider to accept the penis. The penis enlarges and becomes very firm and erect, enabling the man to penetrate deeply into the vagina.

Sexual stimulation causes an increase in vaginal secretions that lubricate the vaginal passage and make it easier for the penis to penetrate. On occasion, however, lubrication may not extend to the labia or external genital area. At such times, the man or woman can use their fingers to draw vaginal lubricating fluid toward the vaginal opening.

The Curve of Excitation. As arousal becomes intense, the entire nervous system becomes involved. Pressure on sensitive nerve endings in the genitals creates the distinctive, mixed sensation of pleasure and discomfort characteristic of sexual arousal. The woman is psychologically prepared, open, and eager to receive the man; the man's whole being is concentrated and focused, ready to enter into and give himself to the woman.

The man may reach intense physical and psychological arousal more quickly than the woman. Neither need become worried about the different physiological and psychological time clock of the other. Attention to foreplay, interest in the other's arousal, teasing, playfulness, and patience all contribute to mutual stimulation and satisfaction. If stimulation continues, the urge for relief becomes dominant. Because relief can be obtained by genital contact and friction, intercourse follows as the natural culmination of intense mutual stimulation. By providing maximum genital contact and friction, intercourse is designed to raise sexual excitement to a peak, or "climax," called orgasm, which is followed by relief and relaxation of tension.

The Orgasm. In other words, when excitement is quite intense, and both partners feel ready, the man inserts his penis into the vagina. Often it is helpful if the woman guides him in this movement. Both partners normally engage in a series of rhythmic, thrusting motions of the pelvis to increase pleasurable contact and friction. These movements, which may last a few seconds or several minutes, cause the physical and emotional excitement to build to a final "climax," at which moment nervous tension is released in orgasm. As the penis spurts seminal fluid into the vagina, the man experiences ejaculation and release of tension, which are his highest excitement and greatest physical pleasure in sexual union. In the woman, spasmodic contractions of the genital muscles and body may vary from highly spasmodic to almost imperceptible.

Male and female orgasms result in the relaxation of the genital blood vessels that maintain erection and tumescence; relief from genital congestion quickly follows. If stimulation is stopped short of orgasm, however, relief occurs very slowly. In some women, such relief may take an hour or more.

Orgasm occurs consistently in the man; it is always definite, obvious, and associated with the movement of ejaculation. Once ejaculation begins, it continues automatically, and it is usually beyond the man's control to stop it. The pattern of orgasm in the woman is more varied. She may experience different responses at different times. Some responses are quite marked and intense, with automatic muscular spasms in the pelvic regions; some are less intense and sometimes imperceptible. A woman's orgasm is not always so definite or localized as a man's. Sometimes it may be a more diffuse reaction of well-being, satisfaction, and intimate union.

For some women, a marked orgasm is infrequent in early marriage and may not occur at all until after months of experience. Moreover, the fact that the woman has experienced intense orgasm several times is no assurance that her response on all subsequent occasions will be similar. On the other hand, the woman, unlike the man, may experience orgasmic reaction more than once, and perhaps several times, in the same period of love-making. Although the man will consistently have an orgasm unless exhausted or preoccupied, he, like the woman, will respond differently, depending on the mood and the circumstances.

Although a young husband may often reach orgasm quite soon after intromission, his ability to maintain an erection and prolong intercourse will increase with experience. This may mean that the woman will often not reach orgasm at the same time the man does. Any stimulation that she finds pleasurable and that helps her achieve orgasm is important to the culmination of sexual fulfillment for both partners.

Sometimes, in the excitement of initital love-making, a young man might experience ejaculation *before* intromission takes place or immediately afterwards. This is not unusual and should cause no embarrassment or anxiety. If premature ejaculation does occur, the couple should recognize the body's ability to recover and realize that after waiting anywhere from a few minutes to several hours, the process of arousal can be initiated again.

With experience and communication, the couple learns the kind and amount of preliminary stimulation each requires to achieve deep physical and emotional release. As experience grows, the couple learns more about "timing" and will sometimes be able to reach orgasm more or less together. Beware, however, of writings that tout an unrealistic "ideal" of consistent, intense, simultaneous orgasm. This experience isn't as easy or as necessary for deep mutual satisfaction as some authors maintain.

Recent extensive publicity given to feminine orgasm may have resulted in overemphasis on this measure of sexual "success." Unfortunately, this can create anxiety in the man (can he cause it?) and in the woman (can she produce it?). Such anxiety can defeat the joy of mutual satisfaction.

THE PSYCHOLOGY OF SEX AND SENSUALITY

Foreplay. Certain areas of the body are especially responsive to sexual stimulation. The mouth, the lips, the genital organs and the areas around them, and a woman's breasts, are the primary areas that are sensitive and capable of arousing sexual feeling. People and moods vary. For some, the ears, neck, shoulders, back, legs, etc., may also be quite sensitive. Stimulation of all these areas by rubbing, fondling, stroking, and kissing gradually produces stronger physical and emotional arousal. Excitement and sexual tension increase.

In "foreplay," no areas of the body are forbidden, and there is no right or wrong. Whatever actions are desired and pleasurable are appropriate. A combination of passion, consideration, sensitivity, and tenderness should accompany foreplay. Both the husband and wife should do all they can to stimulate and increase the partner's pleasure and excitement. For the male, whose body is stimulated quickly and intensely, it is not always easy to prolong love-making and foreplay. For the woman, whose sexual pleasure is greatly enhanced by prolonged foreplay, and whose body may respond to sexual arousal more slowly, it is sometimes frustrating to have sexual activity end quickly. A couple who is able to tell each other what their needs are, who can learn to respond to those needs and prolong love-making and sexual stimulation, can learn not to concentrate on achieving their own orgasms with too much determination.

The mutual tenderness, concern, thoughtfulness, and physical closeness displayed in love-making proves much more assuring, supportive, and meaningful than the act of intercourse itself. When a couple joins physically to fulfill their love, the concern each has for the other's physical pleasure and emotional fulfillment will enrich and enhance their own pleasure and fulfillment.

Sensitivity. Couples in love yearn for unity and openness. They exchange gifts, symbols of their love and sharing. When apart, they spend time on the phone, trying to bridge their separateness. When together, physical expressions of affection—a touch, an embrace, a kiss, a caress—become more frequent and intense, preparing the mind, feelings, and body for total physical love-making.

Overcoming early awkwardness and discovering how to please each other is an intimate experience that binds couples closely together. Beauty and excitement accompany first encounters in love-making, and there is something special about that first, tentative kiss which you will always remember. So it is with love-making in marriage. It involves a dimension of art and skill that comes only with experience and sensitivity.

When eager, trusting, and sensitive to each other's needs and demands, a young couple can experience the wonder of their love as it overflows into new emotions and experiences. Together they are capable of deep physical and emotional response and involvement. Neither should be startled by the fervor—or the timidity—of the other's approach; by the intensity of their own or the partner's response; or even by the changing roles that each will assume at different times in love-making.

As your sexual life continues and patterns of arousal are established, as you learn what pleases and turns the other on, repetition of familiar patterns of sexual arousal will be comfortable and exciting. Variety, on the other hand, is just as, if not more exciting and keeps your sexual relationship stimulating and rewarding. Love-making that is too patterned and rigid can make sexual relations dull and burdensome.

Mood and Atmosphere. The psychological context in which intercourse takes place is important and can vary. Mood and setting; dress; the time of day; privacy; the freedom to proceed in an unhurried manner; music; lighting; the room itself; romantic and seductive words—all provide a special aura that enhances a couple's mutual enjoyment. When the mood of the day has been warm and loving, when you've worked together on a project and are feeling psychologically close, intercourse is a celebration of your loving friendship. Sexual relations can also be satisfying when you have quarreled or when the day has been especially difficult, for now your love-making represents reconciliation and the affirmation of love.

Visual stimulation can also be very important and exciting to the mood of love. Appearance, dress, the gradual disclosure of the body, postures, and positions are all part of the human approach to sexual and sensual fulfillment. Nudity in love-making is natural and normal. What form bodily exposure takes—matter-of-fact, playful, seductive, candid—is entirely up to the couple, and any form is chaste and good. Chastity is "the reasonable use of our sexual powers according to the goals of our state in life." Obviously, then, chastity for the married couple implies full, free, and passionate involvement with each other in all sexual activities that enhance the goals of love and life.

Not being in the mood is sometimes the result of confusion. One partner cannot tell whether the other is interested. Sensitive and not wanting to push, neither gives strong signals about his or her desires, and both might become confused and frustrated. Clear signaling about sexual desires is important.

At other times, fatigue, preoccupation, and anxiety will affect even the most enthusiastic of sexual partners. Each of you has to be sensitive to the many moods and changing needs of your partner. Anxiety may be the worst enemy of sexual enjoyment, especially during periods of strain and stress. It is during these difficult moments that sensitivity to each other's needs and honest communication with one another are necessary.

Communication. Throughout arousal, communication, which varies with individuals, is important. Some desire more, some less communication. Communication does not mean that one partner gives the other detailed instructions; communication means that both partners suggest and acknowledge, through words or sounds, that certain actions are pleasing. These words and sounds reassure and stimulate both partners.

Discuss your love-making. Express your feelings, preferences, thoughts, and problems. Be gentle with each other, for each of you invests a great deal of yourself and your egos in your sexual relationship. Any criticism can be quite hurtful, because when your partner discloses feelings of sexuality, he or she displays a deep trust.

Frequency. Of course, no general rule on the frequency of sexual relations applies. Frequency varies with mood, temperament, health, age, opportunity, etc. Some couples have relations on a fairly regular basis, while for others it is largely a matter of mood and impulse. In the early days and years of marriage, the newness and excitement of sexual relations and involvement will probably stimulate more sexual contact than in later years.

The duration of sexual relations is also a matter of mood and preference. Sometimes, if both partners are in a special state of readiness, sexual activity may culminate in a matter of minutes. At other times, the pace is slower, and an hour or more might not be too long. Remember, there is no scorekeeper in your bedroom marking you on frequency or performance. As you learn to recognize each other's needs and desires, mutually satisfactory patterns will emerge. Occasionally, one partner, who is not "in the mood," may participate in intercourse in a non-passionate, though affectionate way. This is understandable and acceptable. However, a monologue with a passive listener, even though a loving one, is a poor substitute for animated conversations. "Thou shalt not be tepid" is a basic marital guideline.

Techniques. Some knowledge of the basic physiology and techniques of sexual intercourse is necessary and useful. Without this knowledge, ignorance or clumsiness can create problems. On the other hand, undue preoccupation with detailed and intricate techniques of intercourse is not only unnecessary, but can be detrimental if it leads one to take a mechanistic approach to something that expresses feeling. The amount of sensual pleasure that can be produced is not necessaily the most important element in sexual relations, and every possible source of excitation need not be explored systematically. Human love-making is not a blind, animal instinct. Men and women must think about how and with whom to create love. For love-making is just that—creating and expressing love. You cannot substitute mechanical skills for real feelings very long.

SOME OLD MYTHS

Sex is Evil. For many centuries, sex, even marital sex, was thought to be evil. Unfortunately, even in this day and age, some people still think that way. Some ask, "If sex is bad, how can it be made good by a wedding ceremony?"

What a foolish question! *Sex is good.* Full sexual activity always involves a relationship between persons, and the use of sex is thus inherently moral. However, certain ideals and laws limit its use before marriage because of the power of sex and the lack of maturity of most young people. These young people often mistake passion and desire for love and bring harm to themselves and others. Premarital safeguards channel sexual expression toward its noblest use as an integral part of a committed love relationship. The young person who gets sexually involved too soon, too often, can easily develop the attitude that chase, conquest, kicks, and physical performance are all that sex is about. He or she is prevented from ever discovering true sexuality with its rich love dimension.

Knowledge of sex and masculinity go hand in hand. For too long, knowing *all* about sex has been equated with "real" masculinity. Two negative consequences could result from belief in this statement. That is, some men could begin to believe they really know all there is to know and stop trying to be satisfying lovers to their wives. Or, some men could begin to resent or simply ignore their wives' requests, suggestions, or initiative in love-making because they represent a threat to the man's image.

Male and female attitudes and responses to love-making are significantly different. Young men usually respond to sexual stimulation much more rapidly than women, and they may be deeply aroused by even mild stimuli of sight, sound, and touch. Women are less quickly stimulated by what they see, but respond quickly to touch and physical contact.

These statements are broad generalizations, and it would be foolish to say that all men are the same and all women the same. Individual men and women differ greatly. Young couples should *learn their partners* and not assume that he or she fits neatly into a preconceived pattern, or that his or her reactions are "just like mine."

Intense, simultaneous orgasm should be the ideal. Writers who idealize wild, simultaneous orgasm do a disservice. Couples might read these descriptions and question their sex life. "Something's wrong with us; we're falling short."

Chasing after and never achieving some magic, simultaneous orgasm that involves a reaction roughly equivalent to a nuclear explosion can make you feel inferior and inhibit your sexual enjoyment. Sexual intercourse is a form of human expression, and like conversation, it can be animated or subdued, profound or frivolous, dramatic or matter-of-fact. If it suits your mood, it will be highly satisfying.

Any couple with positive attitudes toward sex and consideration for enhancing their mutual pleasure will soon discover the various responses and positions that are most satisfying to them at different times, under different circumstances. If the purpose of the human expression of love is served, any form that the expression takes is good and wholesome.

Sex is in danger. These days, the greatest danger that besets God's gift of sexuality is not that men and women will enjoy it too much, but that *they may make it trivial or commonplace or talk it to death.* When someone on a late night TV show explains six ways to increase sexual pleasure while "making love" under water, sex itself in being harmed. Sex is being taken out of the realm of a rich, personal, human symbol and turned into an exercise in gymnastics. It could soon contain all the excitement of a limp handshake, if not protected and nurtured. Sex will be a most satisfying dimension of your marriage, provided you do not demand too much too soon of marriage, of yourselves, of each other, or of sexuality.

THE WONDER OF SEXUALITY

Your attitudes toward sex, your sexuality, and the sexuality and sensuality of your partner will have a lasting influence on the pleasure you derive from and the joy you bestow on one another in your sexual relationship. As one couple thoughtfully said,

> "In this most intimate and private of human acts, we reveal ourselves to each other, we give ourselves to each other, we join our excited bodies and soaring spirits—our lives and our beings—in passion and joy. In this bed, today and through a thousand tomorrows, we dramatize and celebrate our pledge, our willingness to serve, pleasure, nurture, and heal each other—now and forever."

"The lithe, handsome youth ran swiftly over the fields to the dwelling of his beloved. He knocked vigorously, and to her question, "Who is it?', cried, 'It is thy lover!' The door remained barred. Crestfallen, he withdrew to meditate.

Hours later at evening he returned, this time to tap gently at the door. When her question came again, 'Who is it?', he whispered, 'It is thyself,' and was immediately admitted to her embrace."

Arabian Legend

By its very nature, conjugal love is doubly creative: It calls forth the fullest development of husband and wife as distinctive masculine and feminine images of God; and it produces, through the creation of a child, a captivating, living symbol of their love.

PARENTING

One of the bittersweet things about parental love is that children live in the house of tomorrow, into which parents cannot go. Having accepted the challenge of raising strong Christian persons and wholesome, upright citizens in a changing, far from perfect world, Christian parents also accept the responsibility to work toward bettering the human condition within that world. From their parents, children acquire the basic beliefs, values, and attitudes that shape their lives, their minds, and their futures. Parents are thus a significant part of their children who live in the house of tomorrow. They are accountable not only for their own children, but for their children's children as well. Parenthood is an investment in the present and in the future. A process that lasts for many years, parenting involves nurturing, caring for, loving, and growing with children until they become fully prepared to face life on their own.

SHOULD YOU HAVE CHILDREN?

Contemporary concern about the growth and happiness of the marriage partners and the enrichment of their relationship is appropriate and long overdue. Yet, emphasis on the partnership should not overshadow the importance of the role that marriage plays in the service of new life. Marriage, of course, is not biologically necessary to produce babies. Marriage, however, *is* necessary for procreation to be undertaken in its fullest human sense.

Don't be influenced by environmentalists who would frighten you into believing that children are a form of pollution. We certainly must learn to cherish, conserve, and share the resources that God has given us. Moreover, because of their individual condition and circumstances, couples may appropriately choose to limit family size. However, the general assumption that children are a nasty burden to be avoided is utterly shallow. To devalue the merits of children in the family goes against every basic human principle. Eric Erickson, the great psychiatrist, in outlining the stages of human development, points out that *identity,* achieved during childhood and early adolescence in the family, prepares us for mature *intimacy and relationship.* This in turn, leads us to *creativity and fruitfulness,* the final stage of human development in which we recognize what we can and must give to the future of society by having and rearing children.

Some couples say, "We can't bring children into a world like this." Certainly anyone who does not recognize the serious problems that exist in our world is an ostrich. However, anyone who does not believe that the future can be better, knows no history, does not really believe that Christ and His grace are operating within us, and has not yet learned that one of the great gifts that children and the young possess is hope—the ability to dream the impossible dream and make it come true. While your children move on to a better life tomorrow, the serious problems about which you grieved will take their place in history. Your children will face different problems and begin to fear the effects on their own children, your grandchildren.

Others say, "Children cost money, tie you down, and take away the freedom required to live life to its fullest. Keep your options open." But, living is making choices; becoming mature means choosing wisely. To make definitive choices, you must commit yourself to them and leave other options behind. Only the immature think they can be and do everything. Although having children means cutting off certain options and accepting certain limitations, it also means that you determine to seek mature fulfillment by focusing on and committing your lives toward founding your own family. The rewards are countless. "There is a time for all things under the sun." Marriage is a time for new life, for moving toward the mature, deep relationship of parenthood.

By leading parents into new dimensions of love, children give parents more than they receive. Children can call forth new talents and strengths from parents and bring them to higher levels of human understanding and unselfishness. The challenge of raising children helps to mature and to perfect the personalities of parents. Children give parents a hold on the future. They move them, in a special way, into the community of church, schools, neighborhood, organizations, and society at large.

For many couples, children come and carry them into new stages and involvement in life and love at just about the time that the excitement of early romance has tempered somewhat. In their common concern for the child, the couple shares dreams, plans, pride, and a thousand joys—yes, and disappointment and tears, too. Parenthood is a basic task of husbands and wives wherein they weave a stronger bond of love for each other as they relate to their children. Some say parental love is closest to the selflessness of God's love. Children never fully reciprocate the love that parents have given them, and parents should know this. The child's destiny is to carry the love he or she has received into the future and bestow it on others—upon his or her own children from generation to generation.

Although you cannot and should not expect your love for your children to be fully reciprocated, children are their own reward. Watching a child develop and grow and witnessing his or her delight at the smallest new discovery calls forth unparalleled feelings of pride and satisfaction. Both parents and grandparents derive tremendous pleasure from their children. Children have the capacity to create and sustain great joy.

Just as children can elicit tremendous joy in your lives, so they can elicit great sorrow. Parental efforts and sacrifices must be put forth in rearing children. But the very effort put into comforting, worrying, teaching, feeding, and clothing children is an experience of growth for those who choose to become parents. They become more loving, gentle, patient, giving, and self-sacrificing; they become stronger and wiser too. Children are gifts from God who give each parent the opportunity to become the person he or she would like to become.

When parents witness each other as parents, each develops a greater dimension of respect for the other. No other aspect of married life demands the teamwork that rearing children demands. Parents must work, worry, care, and plan together, and the teamwork brings them closer to and deepens their love for one another. Children can foster and enhance love. By denying yourself the opportunity to have and raise children, you can deny yourself joy and the opportunity for development, progress, and growth. The family will always be the basic unit of society; the loving closeness of a family is nourishing to the child, while the presence of children can foster and promote parental personal growth and development.

THEORY VERSUS PRACTICE

No matter how well you may be prepared for marriage and family, you can be assured that the personal experience of parenthood is quite different from what you expect. Like most human experiences, personal involvement in parenthood modifies your perspective and frequently hinders sound judgment. You may be well-versed in the theory of child-rearing, but you will probably forget all your theories when your first child arrives. For this reason, you may find it helpful to give some thought to the following points.

ADJUSTING TO THE NEW ARRIVAL

The arrival of the first child is a significant event that normally changes a couple's life and involves some redefinition of marital roles. Because the inexperienced young mother must devote a large portion of her time, energy, and attention to the care of the child, she might forget to pay adequate attention to her husband. The young husband might interpret this as willful neglect and come to resent the child as a rival for his wife's affection.

Of course some husbands still feel that bearing and raising children should be consigned entirely to women; they want no part of it. Some wives can unwittingly promote this view by acting as if pregnancy were wholly a woman's affair and confiding only in their mothers or women friends. An intelligent wife realizes that her husband will become a father largely through her efforts. Before the child is born, she prudently relates to "our" pregnancy, sharing her hopes and feelings with him. After the child is born, the wife carefully associates the husband with "our" baby, so he comes to understand and learns to accept the demands of his new role as father.

In the early stages of parenthood, a couple's social life is restricted to some extent. However, it is not necessary to limit it unduly. Although hesitation to leave the new infant is a usual phenomenon of new parents, you owe it to yourselves and your relationship to begin to go out together and build trust in a competent sitter or family member. If you don't take time for yourselves together, it is likely, and understandable, that a pattern of separateness will develop—the wife home with the infant, the husband out alone, or both of you always home and resentful of the confinement.

Each of you must be aware of the other's needs—help each other as much as possible; enjoy the baby together as often as you can; and, most especially, enjoy your precious moments alone with each other.

ADJUSTING TO PARENTAL RESPONSIBILITIES

Children may divide a couple as well as unite them. You and your partner might not agree on child-rearing techniques, and such disagreement can have serious consequences for your marriage and for the welfare of your children. If you differ greatly, keep the following points in mind.

• Never air serious disagreements in the presence of children. Not only will this confuse them, but they will soon learn to play one of you against the other.
• Once you agree on an approach, be loyal and consistent. Although some partners might readily agree to a

program, pressure from the children often causes them to undermine the approach by granting exceptions.

- Don't try to "pass the buck" on your moral responsibilities as parents. If you dare to bring children into the world, you are responsible before God for their loving nurture, religious training, and moral formation, as well as for the supervision of their entertainment and cross-sex associations and the development of their Christian consciences in such matters. Sending your children to Catholic schools does not free you from this responsibility, nor do social pressures to disregard the Christian obligations in your lives.

For Good or Ill, You are Models. Because children acquire their basic beliefs, values, and attitudes by imitating those whom they love and admire, you, as parents, are their most significant models. Whether you like it or not, your example will produce a profound, lasting impression that powerfully overshadows anything they might be taught in school. Day after day, in your actions, casual conversations, formal expressions of opinion, and routine comments, you will reveal your beliefs, values, attitudes, and feelings about religion, politics, neighbors, race relations, and family problems. You will shape the admiring, receptive minds of your children accordingly. This is the "communication of minds...with all the seriousness, delicacy, and selflessness it requires," that Pope Pius XII called the chief trait of parenthood. Considering how severely our Lord chastised anyone who scandalized one of his little ones, you can easily understand why parenthood is a vocation to sanctity.

CHANGING PARENTAL ROLES

"Growing up" is a gradual process, during which children progress toward maturity as they pass through several more or less clearly defined developmental stages. Each stage of development should prepare the child for the next, so that growth will be gradual and continuous. Each of your children will develop at different rates, and you will be able to anticipate their needs for additional knowledge and guidance only if you know how rapidly they are progressing. This will require considerable understanding, foresight, and planning on your part.

From the child's viewpoint, growing up primarily consists of moving from the protective, wholly dependent family milieu to the unprotected, competitive, and increasingly complex environments of the neighborhood, school, peer group, and adult world. As they grow, children must develop their independence, learn to stand on their own two feet, and assume responsibility for their actions. Although you might fear that your children are "growing away" from you, you must accept and encourage the physical and psychic separation required to foster maturity.

WHAT IF YOU CAN'T HAVE CHILDREN?

Perhaps no one has stronger feelings about having children than couples who are involuntarily childless because of infertility. Such infertility was once referred to as "sterility," but thanks to advances in the medical and biological sciences, we now know that people cannot be divided into groups as "fertile" or "sterile." Modern research findings show that fertility is a relative condition for both men and women. Some individuals are highly fertile, some comparatively fertile, while others are sterile.

We do not know the percentage of involuntarily childless married couples in this country, but population experts estimate it to be about 10%. The causes of infertility are multiple; some are still unknown.

Contrary to folklore and myths, the woman is no longer regarded as the major cause of infertility. Current research findings clearly indicate not only that either the husband or the wife can be infertile, but, above all, that a complex combination of causes may account for childlessness in any given couple. Many infertile couples may now obtain medical assistance in achieving their desired goal of pregnancy.

At any rate, no stigma or blame should be attached to the problem of infertility. If you suspect that you are infertile, you should consult a physician as a couple. If you take a positive approach to solving the problem together, the odds are that you will succeed and be rewarded for your mutual efforts.

ADOPTION

If you want children but are unable to do so despite thorough consultation with a qualified specialist, adoption may be the answer. Be aware, however, of the fact that fewer babies are available for adoption because of the increased incidence of birth control, abortion, and unwed mothers who keep their children. Adoption is not as simple or quick as it may have been thirty years ago. The day of crowded orphanages and babies waiting to be adopted have passed; many agencies have long waiting lists of qualified parents. Although adoption is not necessarily an easy solution to the problem of infertility, it is a good and beautiful solution.

If you decide to adopt, it can be just as beautiful, full of love, hope, and promise as pregnancy and birth. The infant or toddler you take into your home will quickly become yours because of the very special type of love that an adopted child summons forth. Adopting a child makes you just as much a parent as giving birth to your own child does. Parent after parent testifies to the joy an adopted child brings to their lives.

HOW DO YOU ADOPT?

Most large Catholic dioceses have licensed agencies (i.e., Catholic Charities) that you can contact to initiate your request for adoption. Other religious groups have their own agencies, and state agencies are also available. All work very hard to find the right home for their children and the right child for the home. A few doctors and lawyers handle adoption cases, and you might prefer to work through them. Whatever route you choose, be prepared to wait. You probably won't regret it.

ALTERNATIVES

After learning that they are apparently infertile, some couples might prefer to remain childless rather than adopt. Those who make this choice can still have lives full of love and hope, but their expression of love will be different from that of parents. Parenting requires great effort, ingenuity, and constant work. A childless couple might direct their energy and ingenuity toward volunteer services, or toward fulfilling, fruitful careers that offer them the opportunity to help, direct, or guide others. Although a Christian marriage, founded on a willing desire to raise a family, implies raising children, it is not the only way to assure that a marriage is loving, Christian, and whole. However, a childless couple must make their marriage whole solely on its own—without benefit of children who call forth love, encourage participation in society, and enhance the entire marital relationship. The childless couple necessarily expends more energy becoming involved with those outside the relationship than the couple with children. Children can bring a depth and breadth to a marriage that no other force can.

"Too many people spend more
time making a living than
they do
living."

MARRIAGE AND MONEY

A young reporter once met the aging John D. Rockefeller, who was sitting alone on a park bench. He asked, "Mr. Rockefeller, what is enough money?"

The elderly tycoon pondered the question for a moment and, then, with a tight smile replied, "Just a little bit more, son. Just a little bit more."

According to researchers, lack of money and the anxiety associated with that lack can be a primary source of stress in marriage. People who have adequate or more than adequate incomes are reported to have happier marriages, mainly because there is less strain on the relationship.

Money has become one of the most basic human motivations. Many covet it; some disdain it; some worry about it constantly; others think it grows on trees. Money can excite strong emotions in all of us. It can mean power, security, control, status, options, and acceptance. Lack of money can produce feelings of inferiority, guilt, helplessness, depression, even anger. We never seem to have enough—both because of the impact of inflation on our income and expenses, as well as our increasing needs and desire for just a little more of the security, power, comfort, and status that money can help provide. More often than not, our expectations continue to outstrip our income. The solution to all this, of course, is either to make a great deal more money, modify our expectations, or plan our budgets carefully.

CONSPICUOUS CONSUMPTION

Our society is geared toward conspicuous consumption. We are bombarded incessantly by the most skillful advertising campaigns that the industry can mount. These campaigns appeal powerfully to our fears, insecurity, greed, and desires. Their motive is profit, their goal to induce us to spend and buy "now." "Brand B cosmetics will make you beautiful." "Type D deodorant will bring you friends." "You deserve XYZ stereo, boat, or snowmobile." "You are 'with it' if you buy Brand C, 'upwardly mobile' if you buy Type E." "You are a 'loser' if you don't have several of Brand A."

The number of young couples who dig themselves into an economic hole because they are unable to wait to purchase something is very large indeed. Once in an economic hole, the stress of not meeting payments mounts, and the bickering about what to buy next continues. That money problems are a significant factor in the dissolution of over 40% of all marriages is not unreasonable when seen from this perspective. Although it might be an unpleasant thought, "less is better" may not be such an unwise axiom. The energy crisis, spiraling costs of consumer items (even absolute necessities), and the diminishing value of the dollar should all indicate that the days when "more of everything is always available" have passed.

ATTITUDES TOWARD MONEY

How you feel about money—the agreement you and your partner reach about how to earn enough money and how to use it—may be vital to harmony in your marriage. Each of you may have developed quite different attitudes toward it. These attitudes should be explored and shared honestly.

For example, although few couples these days question whether the wife will work and may even take it for granted, many couples still struggle with identity crises precipitated by the man's concern that he be primary breadwinner. Open communication about finances and the place each partner has in promoting the security of the relationship should dispel any inner fears or social pressures about specific gender roles.

Just as your backgrounds have influenced your attitudes toward sex, relationships, and personal habits, so too do your backgrounds influence your feelings and attitudes about money. Someone who grew up in poverty and rarely had even the basic necessities of life could easily develop great insecurities about money. This person might need a huge savings account, a piece of land, and an unmortgaged home to feel secure. For him (or her), even minor expenditures on entertainment or frivolity could be threatening. On the other hand, a person from a fairly affluent background might simply take money for granted. He or she might not worry about it and might even spend it foolishly. Of course, the reverse response to each of these life circumstances may be equally possible. Attitude toward money is a matter of values learned and lifestyle chosen based on those values.

Although most of you probably fall somewhere between the two extremes mentioned above, you have picked up definite attitudes toward money. Some of you may have had parents who carried thrift to extremes, viewed money as an end to itself, and enjoyed nothing more than seeing the numbers increase in the savings book. Some of you might have had one parent who kept all the accounts and dispensed the family income, using his or her position to control. Others of you might remember when taking your "allowance" away was a form of punishment, or when receiving money from your parent was conditional upon conforming to ideas and behavior with which you did not agree. Not infrequently, you might find a husband who refuses to tell his wife how much he earns because lack of knowledge keeps her dependent, because he is ashamed he does not earn more, or because he thinks men have a right to freedom with money.

TAKE INVENTORY

Many young couples have a certain *vagueness* about money—where it comes from and where it goes—all of which can lead to debt and worry. You've got to know the territory—exactly where you stand financially—before marriage (for starters). Take inventory and sum up your financial situation. Start by reflecting on your attitudes toward money—"What does money mean to both of us? How have I been influenced by my past experience? What problems do I foresee us having with money?" Jot down your thoughts and write down your assets—cash on hand, savings, securities, equipment, furniture, insurance, any guaranteed increase in income, etc., and list your liabilities, also—bills owed, outstanding loans, installment payments, and the cost of the wedding and the honeymoon.

Do your best to settle as many debts as possible before marriage. Be as candid as you can with each other. Include the $60 you still owe on last year's vacation. Be careful not to forget something or keep it hidden.

BUDGETING—A PROCESS AND A PLAN

After an inventory of assets and liabilities, you should figure out your fixed expenses, that is, what you can expect to spend every month over the next year, which will tell you how much you have to earn to break even. If you're earning more than that, you can begin to think about savings. Most budgeting is hardly high finance. *Money you earn is actually what you have; money you spend is subtracted, and that's it.*

Establish a process for dealing with money matters. Who will handle the money, decide on savings, and pay the bills? Will one of you be chiefly responsible, or will you divide responsibility equally? Will each of you have some amount you can dispose of independently?

Banks and insurance companies distribute booklets on budgets that can stimulate ideas and help you plan a budget that fits your dreams, hopes, and temperaments. Talk long and honestly about your preferences and priorities. See where they fit together, and where compromises have to be made. Establish budgetary goals with which you mutually agree. Consider your budget over time. Your earning capacities will probably increase, but your expenditures will also. The things you consider important will probably change, so build in some flexibility. Allow for emergencies, but don't live in fear of them. Savings put aside on a regular basis can be important, but try not to be so oriented to the future that you miss some of the best years of your lives. On the other hand, try not to be so oriented to the present that you court serious financial problems down the road.

113

As you work out a plan, be sure that it is realistic, otherwise you won't have the motivation to carry it out. Experts suggest you keep careful track of all income and expenditures for the first three to six months to establish a realistic basis for future planning.

BORROWING AND CREDIT

Family Loans. What about loans from your family? Perhaps they can loan money at considerably lower rates than any bank would. Fine. However, if for any reason you doubt that the loan would be treated as a business transaction, it might be better to avoid any potentially emotional encounters with family by not borrowing money from them at all. If you *do* seek assistance from family members or enter into business dealings with them, make sure all arrangements, including appropriate figures, are in a letter of agreement.

Financing. During the first few years, it might be wise to finance the items you need; interest you pay on these debts is an investment in the future. If, on the other hand, you borrow money to buy a car you don't really need, or a boat, or to finance a trip you couldn't otherwise afford, then you may be digging yourself into a financial hole. In the long run, it's cheaper to pay for such items in cash or not purchase them at all.

Credit, whether charge cards, installment purchases, or loans, is not free. Credit is a service, a more convenient way of spacing and stretching payments over time. You pay for this service. Learn precisely what it costs you to buy items on credit. Be sure you understand the additional amount, both in percentages and in dollars and cents. Are you paying credit rates by the month or by the year?. As you pay on the principle, do your rates decrease or remain the same? What is the amount of interest paid over the period of your credit contract? Only when you have these final figures can you make up your mind whether you *really* want to buy now and pay later. Sometimes it makes very good sense; at other times, it's much better to seek alternatives, save your money and pay cash—later.

Credit cards are a wonderful convenience. In the hands of some people, however, they quickly become overheated with use. The ease with which you use them might precipitate a rash of spending that plummets you into debt or gives you a misplaced sense of the realities of your budget situation.

FINAL WORDS

Used wisely, money can contribute to your health, pleasure, ability to give to and share with others, and your future. Handled carefully, your budget can provide a mechanism for mutual planning for the security of your marriage, your future, and the future of your children. Approached with honesty and enthusiasm, budget planning can increase the value of your earnings and give you peace of mind, knowing that spending is within your means and bills can be paid. It won't be easy, but if you both explore your feelings honestly and share the ups and downs of your financial circumstances with understanding and support, you will be well on your way.

"All you people clap your hands and shout for joy. The Lord has made all mankind one. Now let your spirits rise."

CELEBRATE YOUR WEDDING DAY

To celebrate is to demonstrate the meaning of a joyful event. A celebration dramatizes the event with actions, words, rituals, and music that underline and heighten its importance.

Your wedding day is a joyous event for you, your families, and the Christian community. As the beginning of a long adventure, your wedding merits great celebration.

These pages are designed to help you plan your wedding ceremony.

Because contemporary liturgical forms for marriage are quite flexible, you have many options when you select the readings, prayers, and actions you might like to use for your wedding. We encourage you to study the options, discuss them with your parish priest, and fashion a ceremony that will make your wedding day a memorable expression of your unique love for each other.

Individual church parishes have different customs concerning the days or times for holding marriage ceremonies and for musical, floral, and photographic arrangements. The parish priest will explain these customs and apprise you of any special resources that can assist you.

The ideal setting for the sacrament of matrimony is at Mass, the Eucharistic celebration.

An outline of the wedding ceremony and a list of available options follows.

PROCESSION

The ceremony begins with the entrance procession. The priest, attendants, witnesses, parents of the bride, parents of the groom, and others may take part in the procession. Consider the arrangement you prefer and work out a chart for the wedding march. An entrance song is usually sung at this time, but may be replaced by other suitable music.

The bride, groom, and attendants take their assigned places, either within the sanctuary (altar area) or just in front of it, depending on the design of the church and on local custom.

THE LITURGY OF THE WORD

The Mass begins as usual, although you may select one of four different versions of the opening prayer. Each mention the bride and groom by name and ask God's blessing on their love. (See number ONE on page 123. Choose from A, B, C, or D.)

SCRIPTURE READINGS

Three scripture readings are used—one from the Old Testament, one from the Epistles, and the third from the

Gospels. A list of references to the various readings permitted follows. You can, of course, find them in any Bible. Look them up, read them over, and choose the reading in each group that is most meaningful to you.

A variety of very brief responsory prayers and Alleluia verses come between the Epistle and Gospel.

SCRIPTURE SELECTIONS

Old Testament Readings

Genesis 1:26-28, 31a	Male and female He created them.
Genesis 2:18-24	Two in one flesh.
Genesis 24:48-51, 58-67	Isaac loved Rebecca.
Tobit 7:9c-10, 11c-17	May God join you together.
Tobit 8:5-10	May God bring us to old age together.
Song of Songs 2:8-10, 14, 16a; 8:6-7a	Love is strong as death.
Sirach (Ecclesiasticus) 26:1-4, 16-21	Like the sun rising is a good wife.
Jeremiah 31:31-32a, 33-34a	I will make a new covenant.

Epistles

Romans 8:31b-35, 37-39	Who will separate us from Christ's love.
Romans 12:1-2, 9, 18	Offer your bodies as living sacrifice.
1 Corinthians 6-13c, 15a, 17-20	Your body is temple of the Spirit.
1 Corinthians 12:31, 13-8a	Nothing profits without love.
Ephesians 5:2a, 21-33	This mystery of Christ and His Church.
Colossians 3:12-17	Love, the bond of perfection.
1 Peter 3:1-9	Be sympathetic and love the brothers.
1 John 3:18-24	Our love is to be real and active.
1 John 4:7-12	God is love.
Revelation 19:1, 5-9a	Happy those invited to the wedding.

Gospels

Matthew 5:1-12	Rejoice for your reward will be great.
Matthew 5:13-16	The light of the world.
Matthew 7:21, 24-29	The house built on rock.
Matthew 19:3-6	What God has united, man must not divide.
Matthew 22:35-40	The greatest commandment.
Mark 10:6-9	No longer two but one body.
John 2:1-11	The wedding feast at Cana.
John 15:9-12	Remain in my love.
John 15:12-16	My commandment: love one another.
John 17:20-26	May they be completely one.

Note that the first two readings should not be said by a priest. Perhaps the father of the bride and the father of the groom could each read one. Members of the wedding party or other close friends could also be invited to participate.

After the Gospel, the priest will deliver a homily.

THE EXCHANGE OF VOWS

As you know, the priest does not administer the sacrament of matrimony; he is simply the official witness for the Church. By the solemn exchange of vows, the bride and groom bestow the sacrament upon each other.

The priest introduces this part of the ceremony with a short statement on the purpose of marriage. The bride and groom are questioned about their freedom of choice, fidelity to each other, and their acceptance of children. Each is called upon to answer the questions separately.

Listed below are two of the most widely used forms of the marriage vows from which you can choose.

A: I, _____, take you, _____ to be my wife/husband. I promise to be true to you in good times and in bad, in sickness and in health. I will love you and honor you all the days of my life.

B: I, _____, take you, _____, for my lawful wife/husband to have and to hold from this day forward, for better, for worse, for richer, for poorer, in sickness and in health, until death do us part.

After witnessing their consent, the priest blesses the solemn convenant in the name of the people of God.

As long as the key elements outlined here are present, the couple may modify the language of the vows or add elements that are appropriate and have special meanings for them.

BLESSING OF RINGS

The vows may be exchanged with the couple facing the priest, facing each other, or facing the community. The wedding rings are blessed by the priest as an enduring symbol of marriage and are exchanged while the bride and groom recite a further declaration of their love and fidelity. They can choose one of the three prayers shown in number TWO on page 124.

PRAYER OF THE FAITHFUL

Immediately following the ceremony, the entire congregation joins in the prayer of the faithful addressing petitions to God on behalf of the newly married couple. Several forms of this prayer are available; or members of the congregation can express their personal sentiments spontaneously. If you wish, special petitions may be composed for the occasion. Keep in mind the importance of including in these prayers your concern for the needs of the world, the church, the poor, and the suffering.

LITURGY OF THE EUCHARIST

The Mass rite suggests an offertory procession in which the bread and wine are brought to the altar. This could be done by the bride and groom themselves, by parents, members of the wedding, or other predetermined members of the congregation. Three different versions of the "Prayer Over the Gifts" are shown in number THREE on page 124.

The preface follows. Choose the one you prefer from the three prayers listed. (See number FOUR on page 124.)

The mass proceeds as usual until after the congregational recitation of the Our Father. At this point, the solemn nuptial blessing is bestowed by the priest on the newly married couple. Again, three texts are available, and you may choose the one you like. (See number FIVE on page 125.)

PEACE GREETING

The greeting of peace immediately follows the blessing. With some appropriate gesture, such as a handshake, the priest bestows a sign of love and peace upon the bride and groom. At this time, they are invited to exchange a sign with each other...perhaps an embrace or formal kiss. The "peace greeting" is extended to other members of the wedding and to the congregation, again with whatever sign deemed appropriate.

COMMUNION

The newly married couple can receive Holy Communion under both species—the consecrated bread and wine from the chalice. They receive immediately after the priest. You can select one of these optional prayers after communion. (See number SIX on page 126.)

FINAL BLESSING

At the end of Mass, the priest pronounces a final blessing over the couple about to go forth into their life together. There are four optional texts. (See number SEVEN on page 126.) At this point, any local customs, such as the bride presenting her bouquet at the Virgin's altar, would fit.

The ceremony concludes with the recessional.

THE WEDDING WITHOUT THE NUPTIAL MASS

An interfaith couple may prefer a wedding ceremony outside of a Nuptial Mass to lessen any discomfort the non-Catholic partner's family and guests may feel.

The ceremony outside of Mass consists of the procession, opening prayers, and a series of readings called the "Liturgy of the Word." The wedding ceremony takes place after the gospel and the homily. This is followed by the exchange of rings, the prayer of the faithful, and the reading of the nuptial blessing. The rite may be concluded with the recitation of the "Our Father," the bestowal of the final blessing, and the recessional.

OPTIONAL PRAYERS

Choose the one prayer you prefer—A, B, C, or D, when applicable, from each of the following seven sets of prayers.

ONE / **OPENING PRAYER**

A Father, you have made the bond of marriage a holy mystery, a symbol of Christ's love for His Church. Hear our prayers for N. and N. With faith in You and in each other they pledge their love today. May their lives always bear witness to the reality of that love.

B Father, hear our prayers for N. and N. who today are united in marriage before Your altar.
Give them Your blessing, and strengthen their love for each other.

C Father, when You created mankind You willed that man and wife should be one.

Bind N. and N. in the loving union of marriage; and make their love fruitful so that they may be living witnesses to Your divine love in the world.

D Almighty God, hear our prayers for N. and N. who have come here today to be united in the sacrament of marriage.

Increase their faith in You and in each other, and through them bless Your Church (with Christian children).

TWO / **BLESSING OF RINGS**

A Lord, bless + and consecrate N. and N. in their love for each other. May these rings be a symbol of true faith in each other, and always remind them of their love.

B May the Lord bless + these rings which you give to each other as the sign of your love and fidelity.

C Lord, bless these rings which we bless + in Your name. Grant that those who wear them may always have a deep faith in each other. May they do Your will and always live together in peace, good will, and love.

THREE / **PRAYER OVER THE GIFTS**

A Lord, accept our offering for this newly-married couple, N. and N. By Your love and providence You have brought them together; now bless them all the days of their married life.

B Lord, accept the gifts we offer You on this happy day.
In Your Fatherly love watch over and protect N. and N. whom You have united in marriage.

C Lord, hear our prayers and accept the gifts we offer for N. and N. Today You have made them one in the sacrament of marriage. May the mystery of Christ's unselfish love, which we celebrate in this eucharist, increase their love for You and for each other.

FOUR / **PREFACE**

A Father, all-powerful and ever-loving God, we do well always and everywhere to give You thanks through Jesus Christ our Lord.

Through Him You entered into a new covenant with Your people. You restored man to grace in the saving mystery of redemption. You gave him a share in divine life through his union with Christ. You made him an heir of Christ's eternal glory.

This outpouring of love in the new covenant of grace is symbolized in the marriage covenant that seals the love of husband and wife and reflects Your divine plan of love. And so, with the angels and all the saints in heaven we proclaim Your glory and join their unending hymn of praise.

B Father, all-powerful and ever-living God, we do well always and everywhere to give You thanks. By this sacrament Your grace unites man and woman in an unbreakable bond of love and peace.

You have designed the chaste love of husband and wife for the increase of the human family and of Your own family born in baptism.

You are the loving Father of the world of nature; You are the loving Father of the new creation of grace. In Christian marriage You bring together the two orders of creation: Nature's gift of children enriches the world. Your grace enriches Your Church.

Through Christ the choirs of angels and all the saints praise and worship Your glory. May our voices blend with theirs as we join in their unending hymn.

C Father, all-powerful, and ever-living God, we do well always and everywhere to give You thanks.

You created man in love to share Your divine life. We see His high destiny in the love of husband and wife, which bears the imprint of Your own divine love.

Love is man's origin, love is his constant calling, love is his fulfillment in heaven.

The love of man and woman is made holy in the sacrament of marriage, and becomes the mirror of Your everlasting love.

Through Christ the choirs of angels and all the saints praise and worship Your glory. May our voices blend with theirs as we join in their unending hymn.

FIVE / **NUPTIAL BLESSING**

A My dear friends, let us turn to the Lord and pray that He will bless with His grace this woman (or N.) now married in Christ to this man (or N.) and that (through the sacrament of the body and blood of Christ) He will unite in love the couple He has joined in this holy bond.

Father, by Your power You have made everything out of nothing. In the beginning You created the universe and made mankind in Your own likeness. You gave man the constant help of woman so that man and woman should no longer be two, but one flesh, and You teach us that what You have united may never be divided.

Father, You have made the union of man and wife so holy a mystery that it symbolizes the marriage of Christ and His Church.

Father, by Your plan man and woman are united, and married life has been established as the one blessing that was not forfeited by original sin or washed away in the flood.

Look with love upon this woman, Your daughter, now joined to her husband in marriage. She asks Your blessing. Give her the grace of love and peace. May she always follow the example of the holy women whose praises are sung in the scriptures.

May her husband put his trust in her and recognize that she is his equal and heir with him to the life of grace. May he always honor her and love her as Christ loves His bride, the Church.

Father, keep them always true to Your commandments. Keep them faithful in marriage and let them be living examples of Christian life.

Give them the strength which comes from the gospel so that they may be witnesses of Christ to others. (Bless them with children and help them to be good parents. May they live to see their children's children.) And, after a happy old age, grant them fullness of life with the saints in the kingdom of heaven.

B Let us pray to the Lord for N. and N. who come to God's altar at the beginning of their married life so that they may always be united in love for each other (as they now share in the body and blood of Christ).

Holy Father, You created mankind in Your own image and made man and woman to be joined as husband and wife in union of body and heart and so fulfill their mission in this world.

Father, to reveal the plan of Your love, You made the union of husband and wife an image of the covenant between You and Your people. In the fulfillment of this sacrament, the marriage of Christian man and woman is a sign of the marriage between Christ and Church. Father, stretch our Your hand, and bless N. and N.

Lord, grant that as they begin to live this sacrament they may share with each other the gifts of Your love, and become one in heart and mind, as witnesses to Your presence in their marriage. Help them to create a home together (and give them children to be formed by the gospel who will have a place in Your family).

Give Your blessings to (N.) Your daughter, may she be a good wife and mother, caring for the home, faithful in love for her husband, generous and kind. Give Your blessings to (N.) Your son, so that he may be a faithful husband and a good father.

Father, grant that as they come together to Your table on earth, so they may one day have the joy of sharing Your feast in heaven.

C My dear friends, let us ask God for His continued blessings upon this bridegroom and his bride (or N. and N.).

Holy Father, creator of the universe, maker of man and woman in Your own likeness, source of blessing for married life, we humbly pray to You for this woman who today is united with her husband in the sacrament of marriage.

May Your fullest blessing come upon her and her husband so that together they may rejoice in Your gift of married love (and enrich Your Church with their children).

Lord, may they both praise You when they are happy and turn to You in their sorrows. May they be glad that You help them in their need.

May they pray to You in the community of the Church, and be Your witnesses in the world. May they reach old age in the company of their friends, and come at last to the kingdom of heaven.

SIX / **PRAYER AFTER COMMUNION**

A Lord, in Your love You have given us this eucharist to unite us with one another and with You. As You have made N. and N. one in this sacrament of marriage (and in the sharing of the one bread and the one cup), so now make them one in love for each other.

B Lord, we who have shared the food of Your table pray for our friends N. and N. whom You have joined together in marriage. Keep them close always. May their love for each other proclaim to all the world their faith in You.

C Almighty God, may the sacrifice we have offered and the eucharist we have shared strengthen the love of N. and N., and give us all Your Fatherly aid.

SEVEN / **FINAL BLESSING**

A May the Lord Jesus, Who was guest at the wedding in Cana, bless you in your families and your friends. Amen.

May Jesus, Who loved His Church to the very end fill your hearts with His love always. Amen.